THE
RELUCTANT
WARRIORS

THE
RELUCTANT
WARRIORS

❀ ❀ ❀ ❀

DONALD ARMSTRONG

Brigadier General, U.S. Army, Ret.

THOMAS Y. CROWELL COMPANY

New York, Established 1834

To the memory of my father,
Samuel Treat Armstrong, M.D., Ph.D.,
who taught me to appreciate
the Greek and Roman historians.

Excerpts from *Appian's Roman History*, I, translated by Horace White, and *Polybius*, VI, translated by W. R. Paton, are reprinted by permission of Harvard University Press, Cambridge, Mass., and William Heinemann, London, and The Loeb Classical Library.

Designed by Laurel Wagner
Manufactured in the United States of America
L.C. Card 66-22415
1 2 3 4 5 6 7 8 9 10

PREFACE

This book is about the third and last of the Punic Wars between Rome and Carthage and the events which led up to it. This conflict, which capped a 118-year struggle for control of the ancient Mediterranean world, lasted from 149 to 146 B.C.

The final Punic War has been neglected by most historians. Attracted by the genius of the Carthaginian commander Hannibal, they have preferred to study the Second Punic War, also known as the Hannibalic War. The resulting eclipse of the third war is unfortunate because the last years of Carthage were highly dramatic, and the war itself is unique in history. It was a contest between two powers with directly opposed motivations: militaristic Rome had an inordinate desire to dominate the world; Carthage, on the other hand, loved peace and was prepared to maintain it at almost any price.

Carthage had abandoned war as an instrument of national policy. In obedience to Rome's command, she surrendered unconditionally and disarmed herself unilaterally. But when Rome, believing Carthage to be helpless, decreed the destruction of the city, the Carthaginians rose in a moment of frenzy and declared war on their tormentor. In one of the strangest upsets in military history, Carthage, which had begun the war with hardly a weapon at hand, triumphed for two years over mighty Rome before finally being defeated. Knowledge of Carthaginian character and behavior and of the heritage the Carthaginians received from Tyre, the analysis of which is the chief purpose of this book's early chapters, should have told the Romans what to expect from their ultimatum.

The Roman pattern of conquest has a startling relevance for our own time. For more than forty years prior to the final conflict, Rome conducted a cold war that weakened Carthage materially and spiritually. This cold war included all the tactics used today by Communist nations against the Free World: proxy warfare, terror, blackmail, psychological warfare, deception, subversion, and propaganda.

Rome did not need this war. Her security was assured by her great superiority in population and by her strong army and navy. Carthage, desiring only to preserve the peace, was no threat, actual or potential, to Rome. Nevertheless, Rome goaded Carthage, a nation of usually reluctant warriors, into becoming a raging enemy. Rome had violated a principle that no one has defined better than Rabelais, when his Gargantua says (Chapter XLIII):

Sound military doctrine teaches us that you must never reduce your enemy to desperation, because such a plight multiplies his force and increases his courage which had already vanished. There is no better help for men who are demoralized and worn out by fatigue than to have no hope of salvation. How many victories have been taken out of the hands of the victorious by the vanquished when the victors were not satisfied with reasonable achievement, but attempted total destruction of the enemy.

Carthage, compared to Rome, was relatively democratic. The Carthaginians maintained civil control over their armed forces through two suffetes, who were elected annually, and the senate, which had the power to declare war and to conduct all public business. The suffetes, unlike the Roman consuls, were never generals in wartime.

Aristotle, in his *Politics* (II, 8), praised the Carthaginian constitution for its "many outstanding features as compared with those of other nations." The proof of its superiority, said Aristotle, was that "neither civil strife has arisen in any degree worth mentioning, nor yet a tyrant."

Of course, Aristotle, who lived from 384 to 322 B.C., was admiring Carthage the city-state, not Carthage the empire-state. The Carthaginian empire always lacked cohesion, as indicated by the defection of Utica and Bizerte to rebellious mercenaries in 239 and by the secession of Utica again in 149. Within Carthage itself, however, the constitution remained effective, despite severe factional disputes that arose throughout her history.

Archaeologists have told us much about Carthage, but far more remains unknown about both the city and its inhabitants. We do not even know the name of the statesman who led Carthage in its final struggle for survival. Certainly, none of the men whose names and actions are known seem to qualify for this role. We can only assume that some unknown leader, a Carthaginian Churchill, must have aroused and maintained the high morale and will to resist that held Rome at bay for three long years.

Little is left of the city itself. Urns containing the charred bones of infants have been found on the site, confirming history's stories of the sacrifice of children to Moloch. Other graves have revealed additional details of Carthaginian life, but few ruins have survived. The most significant remains of the city are its two ports.

Historical records of Carthage are even scantier. No chronicles or literature written by the Carthaginians, whose Phoenician ancestors invented the alphabet, have escaped destruction. Virtually all that is known of the Carthaginians and the Phoenicians is contained in the frequently hostile Old Testament and the writings of Greeks and Romans. All the evidence cited in this book concerning Roman imperialism, injustice, and deception was reported originally by historians friendly to Rome.

I have been interested in the Punic Wars since reading Livy in college in 1905. In 1937, and again in 1960, I visited Cannae and other Hannibalic battlefields. In 1958 and 1960 I visited Tunisia, and it was then that I decided to write this book.

The example of Carthage should not be forgotten. Militaristic nations, such as imperialistic Rome, that have been trained in and encouraged to war, hold lovers of peace in contempt. They appreciate the compliance of peace-loving nations, such as Carthage, for peace at any price makes conquest easier. Invariably the ruthless aggressor also is able to take advantage of other vulnerabilities of the prospective victim, such as internal social or political disunity, an ineffective foreign policy, or an unsound military policy. These are the weaknesses Appian must have had in mind when, commenting on events in 193 B.C., he wrote in *The Syrian Wars* (II, 8) that Carthage "had no firm or consistent policy—the very lack of which caused its destruction not long afterward." Rome profited from these defects in policies, taking particular advantage, for example, of the mistake Carthage made by denying social justice to its neighbors. In waging cold war today, let us remember, therefore, not only the national character and behavior of our adversaries, but let us look to our own policies and to any social, economic, or political conflicts within our boundaries. As the philosopher Santayana has said:

"Those who cannot remember the past are condemned to repeat it."

ACKNOWLEDGMENTS

My indebtedness to those who have written on the Punic Wars and on Rome and Carthage is great, but difficult to particularize since my reading on these subjects has extended over half a century. This book is based almost exclusively on the Greek and Roman historians listed in the Appendix. They have been my constant companions since 1910. Modern books to which I owe my thanks are also listed in the Appendix.

My thanks are due to all those who have assisted me with suggestions and advice and criticism. Among those to whom I am especially indebted are:

Frank R. Barnett, one-time Rhodes scholar at Oxford University, President of the National Strategy Information Center, Inc., and consulting Program Manager for the American Bar Association Standing Committee on Education Against Communism. He hardly ever fails to emphasize in a few paragraphs of his innumerable speeches and articles the lessons of Carthage's preoccupation with business-as-usual and her refusal to believe that Cato meant what he said. Mr. Barnett planted the seed which grew into this book.

Mr. Morris I. Leibman, Chairman of the Standing Committee on Education Against Communism of the American Bar Association, who since 1959 has encouraged me to write this book.

Mr. Robert Strausz-Hupe, Director of the Foreign Policy Research Institute of the University of Pennsylvania, and Colonel William R. Kintner, U.S. Army, Retired, also of the Institute, and Walter F. Hahn, formerly of the Institute, for editorial assistance in the early stages of preparing this book.

Mr. Pierre Cintas, whose guidance in visits to Carthaginian sites near Tunis and in discussions at his home during my second visit in 1960 was of inestimable value in explaining details of Carthaginian history and archaeology.

Mr. Abdelaziz Driss, Curator of the Bardo Museum in Tunis, and M. Hassen Hosni Abdelwahab, Director of the Institut Archeologique of Tunis, who increased my understanding of the Carthaginians and their way of life.

His Excellency the Ambassador of Tunis, Rachid Driss, and M. Ghardi, Cultural Attaché, for much assistance of various kinds.

Mr. Howard I. Chapelle, Curator of Transportation, Smithsonian Institution, Washington, D. C., for his helpful information on ancient ships.

Army Photographic Agency, especially Mrs. Traxler.

Army Map Service, especially Mr. Muck.

Libraries, which together met my needs for books and maps not in my own collection:

Library of Congress

Dumbarton Oaks and the Center for Hellenic Studies, both of Harvard University

National War College, Fort McNair

The University Club Library, New York City

The Cosmos Club Library, Washington, D.C.

I am grateful to Mr. N. J. Anthony, Associate Editor of Army, for his skill in deciphering and typewriting my manuscript, and to Mr. Harvey I. Stailey, Director of Visual Aids, National War College, for the maps. Both worked at night or weekends to meet my deadlines. Any error in the maps is entirely my responsibility as Mr. Stailey followed my instructions to the letter in drawing them.

I am deeply grateful for the editorial assistance of Mr. Henry

ACKNOWLEDGMENTS

Moscow, and of Messrs. Martin Mann and Hugh Rawson of the
Thomas Y. Crowell Company.

But above all I want to record my gratitude to my beloved wife,
Irene Troukhatchoff Armstrong, who started me on the road to
the authorship of this book when we flew to Tunis in 1958, and
accompanied me in its ordeals and adventures until her death on
April 2, 1965. This book is my memorial to her devotion and patience in enduring the thousands of hours I spent in my library
concentrating on the death of Carthage.

I also desire to thank the publishers, Harvard University Press,
Cambridge, Mass. and William Heineman Ltd., London and The
Loeb Classical Library for permission to reprint the extensive
excerpts from Appian and Polybius.

CONTENTS

INTRODUCTION

In the midst of the many problems which confront the nations of the world today, it is sometimes wise to sit back and analyze the problems that other nations have faced in the past, to examine the methods our predecessors have used in attempting to solve their difficulties, and to try to determine what influences caused them to adopt the solutions that they did. There is much to learn from weighing these considerations with the effectiveness of their efforts. [The author of this exciting book has taken us back in history to lessons which should be required reading today.]

Throughout history each nation has been greatly concerned with its own security and prosperity and with the peace and security of the world in general. For centuries governments of all kinds have endeavored to solve the political and economic problems which lie at the root of tension between states. Every nation has adopted policies that it proclaims will further the cause of peace and reduce the probability of war. Statements have been made in every tongue that given good will and honest intentions on the part of all people, even the most difficult international problems can be resolved in a peaceful and equitable manner. New systems of international cooperation have been sought by each generation because each generation seems convinced that the old order is not adequate to cope with the immense political, economic, and technological situations that the new generation has inherited.

Peace is sought. But peace seems never to be secure.

Century after century nations have disavowed aggression as a national policy. Along with repeated reassurances of peaceful intentions and restatements of their goal to create worldwide conditions which would make the use of force impossible, some nations, not all, pursue policies aimed at the elimination of rival nations or at reduction in their power and influence to such an extent that the weakened nation will no longer be able to determine its own destiny or way of life. [As the author points out, rich, powerful nations with high standards of living want only to maintain the status quo; they try their best to avoid conflict and controversies that might lead to conflict. But there always seem to have been some nations that covet the possessions and power of their neighbors. These nations have the definite aim of upsetting the status quo, not by peaceful competition but by destruction and conquest. These nations strive mightily to build up their own aggressive power, using peaceful protestations and artful negotiations to settle differences, as a device to win over noncommitted nations and to mislead those whom they would destroy. They take advantage of every concession to gain yet another concession. They interpret their victims' efforts to maintain the peace, to placate and please, as a sign of weakness and deterioration.]

So it was with prosperous, passive, peaceful Carthage and aggressive Rome.

In the years before the final Punic War, Carthage through her commerce became wealthy again and wanted peace to pursue her even way of life beyond all else. Rome set out to reduce the power and influence of Carthage and eventually to destroy her. Rome succeeded, step by little step, because Carthage placed her complete confidence in the integrity and good faith of the Romans. She was convinced that since war would be expensive to all participants, the Romans would not resort to war since logically it was profitable for them not to do so.

Only it did not work out that way.

To restore peace after defeating Hannibal in the Second Punic War, Rome in 201 B.C. had demanded tribute. Carthage paid annually for the prescribed fifty years.

To prove the peaceful intent of Carthage, Rome demanded the destruction of the Carthaginian fleet. Carthage destroyed her fleet.

To prevent the build-up of a Carthaginian army, Rome required Carthage to promise not to make war without consulting her. Carthage complied.

But in 150 B.C. Masinissa's depredations escalated, with Roman connivance, from guerrilla tactics into the outright siege of a Carthaginian city. Outraged by this act of aggression, Carthage without Rome's permission mobilized an army, which Masinissa eventually destroyed. When in the following year Roman subversion and bribery gained the Carthaginian city of Utica as an ally and base of operations, Rome declared war on Carthage, but promised a Carthaginian armistice delegation to respect their boundaries and their sovereignty. Carthage then surrendered unconditionally.

In 1962 I was unaware that the following sentences concerning our conflict with communism, for publication in *Orbis* (a quarterly journal on foreign policy), applied literally to Rome's procedure against Carthage:

The contemporary struggle, therefore, is not a conventional struggle based solely or even principally on military force. It is a total effort at annihilation of our way of life. This urge for destruction is nourished by a belief in the skillful and ruthless use of total power. Exercising this total power, the communists expect to control events and rewrite history.

Rome *did* control events, and she *did* rewrite history by deleting the Carthaginian people from its subsequent pages. Several preliminary steps, however, remained to be taken:

To prevent Carthaginian resistance or refusal to meet her further requirements, Rome demanded hostages. Carthage gave them.

To prove that Carthage sincerely desired peace, and to make resistance impossible, Rome finally demanded surrender of all arms, and dependence on the Romans for their protection. Carthage complied.

Over the years Carthage sought only to satisfy Rome. What could the Carthaginians pay or do to persuade the Romans to let them live in peace? They met all demands—but that was not enough.

At last Rome notified the fearful, pleading representatives of Carthage that Carthage would be razed to the ground.

Too late—much too late—the Carthaginians realized the significance of their past actions and the end that threatened them and their civilization.

Finally they fought—gallantly, desperately, skillfully—but in vain.

[General Armstrong is apparently the first student of the Punic Wars to observe Rome's employment against Carthage of every cold-war device from a proxy power to propaganda and psychological warfare, all of which we seem to consider modern communist inventions. His book is the first to analyze Rome's strategy of the indirect approach in this ancient example of unconventional war. It is a scholarly work written in a style that not only whets the interest of the reader but enables him to understand what happened as well as why it happened.]

I greatly enjoyed reading his very excellent book.

ARLEIGH BURKE

Admiral, U.S. Navy, Retired.

The Director, The Center for Strategic Studies.

Georgetown University,

Washington, D.C.

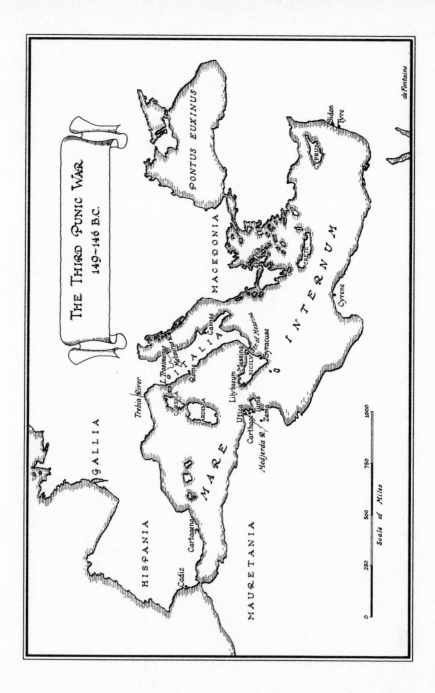

THE THIRD PUNIC WAR
149~146 B.C.

PONTUS EUXINUS

GALLIA

HISPANIA

Cartagena

Codiz

MAURETANIA

CORSICA

SARDINIA

MARE

ITALIA

Trebia River

L. Trasimenus
Metaurus
Rome
Cannae

Lilybaeum
Messina
SICILY Str. of Messina
Syracuse

Utica
Carthage
Tunis
Medjerda R.
Zama

MACEDONIA

INTERNUM

CYPRUS

Sidon
Tyre

Cyrene

Scale of Miles

0   250   500   750   1000

de Fontaine

I

THE BIRTH OF CARTHAGE

As the bustling crews prepared to haul the broad-beamed merchant ships up the beach, the little band of refugees from Tyre poured out a libation of wine in thanks to their gods for having protected them during their year-long, 1500-mile Mediterranean journey. Then they climbed down the landing ladders and assembled around the priests to consecrate the spot where they had put ashore.

Before their stealthy, dead-of-night departure to escape the avarice and tyranny of Tyre's King Pygmalion, they had determined precisely where they wanted to go to found their new home. Their native Phoenicia, of which Tyre was the foremost city-state, had maintained a trading post at Utica on North Africa's coast for three hundred years, and every informed Phoenician knew of the Utica region's allures. The land was fertile but sparsely settled, the climate benign, and the site, a hundred miles southwest of Sicily, superb for commerce and command of the sea. The refugees, led by the beautiful Princess Elissa, or Dido, and including a number of girls recruited during a prolonged stopover on Cyprus, had chosen a place just twenty miles southeast of Utica—and ten miles east of modern Tunis. Now at last they were there.

The refugees had fled soon after the murder of Sychaeus, uncle of Pygmalion, husband of Pygmalion's sister Elissa, and High Priest of Melkart. It had been a peculiarly revolting and

1

abominable crime, in their eyes, for it struck at the very heart
of their religion. Tyre acknowledged many gods, but Melkart
had watched over it for several thousand years, and under his
tutelage the city had prospered splendidly, gaining hegemony
over the other city-states of Phoenicia and even other parts of
Cyprus. The murderer's identity and his motive made things
worse: the killer was Pygmalion himself, and he had slain his
uncle for his wealth. Distraught with grief at the death of her
beloved husband and fearful for her own safety, Elissa had resolved to escape from her ruthless brother, and hatred for
Pygmalion had moved many Tyrian aristocrats to agree to accom-
pany her. So, with Elissa, whose great-aunt was Jezebel, as the
leader, the party had set out surreptitiously in a little fleet of 60-
foot-long trading vessels known for the breadth of their hulls as
"round ships"—to distinguish them from the narrow, swift, and
more maneuverable fighting craft known as "long ships." Whether
Pygmalion sent pursuers to bring them back, history—or even
legend—does not say: presumably, it was a leisurely voyage, with
nightly pauses facilitated by the shallow draft of the vessels,
which permitted them to beach easily in the absence of suitable
harbors. And a year after their flight from Tyre, the refugees
beached their boats for the last time.

The arrival of the newcomers did not alarm the Libyans, a
primitive, seminomadic, non-negroid people who had lived in
that part of North Africa for centuries, tending their flocks and
herds and perhaps doing a little farming. The Libyans knew the
Tyrians well, for Utica's Tyrian merchants sold them wheat, the
olive oil they needed for cooking, lighting, and cosmetic purposes;
amphoras for storing oil, water, and wine; trinkets—which they
loved; and bronze and iron tools and weapons. The Libyans considered the Tyrian trading post not a threat but a blessing.
The newcomers, it is true, differed from Utica's merchants on their

small island in that they wanted to build a city in Libyan territory, but they were so few, and they requested so little. As the historian Appian of Alexandria has written:

They asked for as much land for a dwelling-place as an oxhide would encompass. The Libyans laughed at the paltriness of the Phoenicians' request, and were ashamed to deny so small a favor. Besides, they could not imagine how a town could be built in so narrow a space, and wishing to unravel the subtlety, they agreed to give it, and confirmed the promise by an oath.

One day in the year that we designate 814 B.C., Libyans and Tyrian exiles met to consummate the deal on a hilltop which the Princess and her companions had chosen. The vista was magnificent. A dozen miles away to the east, across sparkling blue water, rose the easternmost peaks of the Atlas Mountains, which stretch 1500 miles over North Africa from Morocco to the promontory now called Cape Bon. The water across which the refugees peered was the Gulf of Tunis, formed by Cape Bon and by Cape Farina, some fifty miles to the west. The only gulf on the North African coast, it offered a welcome haven to sailors. Below the refugees, on either side of an isthmus leading to the mainland, lagoons opened to the gulf. The southerly lagoon could shelter a thousand ships; the other was shallow and sand bars were beginning to make it difficult for vessels to enter.

One of the lower hills in the distance hid from view the settlement of Utica, which lay on an island and owned a harbor where Tyrian merchant ships paused halfway in their voyages to Cadiz, on Spain's Atlantic coast. The hill screened also the only large river in the region; then called the Bagradas (now the Medjerda), it flowed more than two hundred miles from Algeria to empty into the Gulf of Tunis, usually between Utica and the high ground on which the refugees stood. The Bagradas was a torrent in the rainy winter season, a mere trickle in the hot dry

3

summer, but not far from the hill that the refugees had chosen was a spring—which still flows—and cisterns could garner the rainfall; there was enough along the Mediterranean shore (it is 40 inches annually now) to forest the mountainsides.

But most important to the Princess and her advisers were the circumstances that their hill provided a splendid observation point and that, standing on a peninsula, it was well adapted to defense. They had decided it would make a nearly ideal acropolis —a citadel and temple site—for the city they hoped to build, and which they planned to name Kart-Hadasht, "new city" or "new capital" in Phoenician.

The Tyrians' negotiations with the Libyans got off to a friendly start because the Libyan king had already been smitten with the young and charming Princess and because the Libyans were amused by the modesty of the Tyrians' request. Presumably they were less amused when the Tyrians cut the oxhide into thin ribbons and enclosed the whole hilltop. But the Libyans kept their promise, and the Tyrian refugees built their citadel and temple.

Thus were born Carthage and the Carthaginian empire.

So runs the legend. History records only that a King Pygmalion ruled Tyre from 820 to 774 B.C. and that he had a sister Elissa, who came to be called Dido. How much of the rest of the story is myth we cannot know. Concerning the tradition of the oxhide, skeptics point out that since the hilltop was called *bosra*, the Phoenician word for citadel, confusion with the Greek word *bursa* (oxhide) may have given rise to the tale. In any event, the ancient historians all call Carthage's acropolis Byrsa. But the link between Tyre and Carthage is incontestable. M. Pierre Cintas, the eminent authority on Phoenician and Carthaginian archaeology, has discovered on low ground near the commercial port a small sanctuary which he believes marks the spot near which the Tyrian founders of Carthage beached their little fleet, and where they celebrated in later years memorial rites to Elissa.

Whatever the whole truth may be, and however Carthage was founded, Carthage never forgot Tyre and never forswore Tyre's god Melkart. But Melkart and his fellow gods dealt unkindly with Elissa, or Dido, and eventually with Carthage. There are two versions of the lovely Princess's fate, both of them unhappy. Vergil in his *Aeneid* relates that she died by her own hand on a funeral pyre after her wandering lover, Aeneas, sailed away to fulfill his destiny by founding Rome. In the other version, she killed herself to escape the amorous advances of the Libyan king who had granted her the hilltop. Either way, she preferred death to humiliation. And 668 years after she had founded her capital, Carthage itself was to prefer death to humiliation. A heroine as tragic as Elissa, known to history only as the wife of Hasdrubal, hurled her children and then herself from the citadel's summit to avoid Roman captivity—their funeral pyre the flaming city of Carthage itself—and the last defenders died on the hilltop where a ring of massive fortifications had replaced the ribbon of oxhide.

This book will not attempt to recount the history of those 668 years in detail. Its purpose, rather, is to illuminate a little-studied but highly dramatic era replete with parallels to—and lessons for—our own times. The period witnessed a struggle between two great powers with contrasting motivations: militaristic Rome, driven by lust for world dominion, and pacific, commercial-minded Carthage, determined to preserve the *status quo* and to maintain peace at any price. The contest took many shapes. Its varied phases included a cold war in which the weapons were deception, subversion, terror, and blackmail; an experiment in total, unilateral disarmament; and a series of hot wars, the last of which, unique in its origins and in its astonishing upsets, has been virtually ignored by historians. It is this last war—the Third Punic War—with which this book is chiefly concerned.

Before it, Carthage had abandoned war as an instrument of policy and, at Roman command, had disarmed herself. Then Rome pronounced a death sentence upon the city. Weaponless, Carthage unhesitatingly declared war on her persecutor, and in one of the strangest episodes in military annals, for two years triumphed over Roman armed might. No other war has proved so aptly the truth of Napoleon's dictum that in war the moral is to the physical as three to one—until the physical becomes overwhelming. Then Rome locked Carthage in an airtight siege, gaining as allies famine, agony, and death. As flames consumed the city, resistance within it collapsed, and Carthage perished. It had single-mindedly pursued material wealth too long: its final, magnificent defense of liberty and life had come too late, and wealth, liberty, and life all vanished together in the smoke that shrouded the citadel.

II

THE LEGACY OF TYRE

The tragedy of Carthage had its roots in Tyre, and to understand the behavior of the Carthaginians it is necessary to understand something of Tyre and of the world in which Carthage and Tyre prospered.

Tyre was already ancient when Carthage was born. In the very middle of Carthage's life, Herodotus, the Father of History, sailed to Tyre because, as he wrote, he had "heard that there was a very holy temple of Hercules" in the city, and to the Greeks, who often identified foreign gods with their own, Melkart was Hercules by another name. Viewing the temple, so different in style from the temples he knew at home, the ever-questioning Herodotus wanted to know when it had been built. "The temple of the god," the proud priests replied, "was founded when Tyre first became a city and that was two thousand three hundred years hence." Herodotus's visit took place, possibly, about 450 B.C., so if the priests were correct, Herodotus has given us the age of the great Phoenician city from which Carthage sprang.

Phoenicia, corresponding roughly to modern Lebanon, stretched north from Palestine for about two hundred miles along the eastern Mediterranean coast. Like Greece, Italy, and Sicily, Phoenicia comprised many independent city-states, each ruled by its own king and each rarely larger than a small American county. Tyre, though it was the most important of the Phoenician kingdoms, had a perimeter of a mere two and a half miles.

7

It occupied a rocky island about a third of a mile offshore which originally had been two islands: the diligent Phoenicians had filled in a channel between them to build their city.

Despite its limited area, the site was ideal by Phoenician standards, for it promised security and trade facilities, of which the Tyrians made expert use: military engineers enhanced the island's natural defenses by building massive walls and high towers around the rocky shore, and two harbors—one to the north, the other to the south—served freighters and the Tyrian navy. It quickly became a crowded place, so crowded that even though it spilled over onto the mainland, it had to build skyscrapers to shelter its people. Strabo (64 B.C.–A.D. 19) reports that Tyre's houses were "many stories high, even more than the houses at Rome, and on this account, whenever an earthquake took place, it lacked but little of utterly wiping out the city."

Beyond relating that the houses were high, Strabo left no description of them. Neither did other chroniclers, and Tyre today lies in part deep below the modern, much smaller town of Sur and in part submerged in the sea, into which one of the two original islands, the Island of Melkart, long ago sank. But it is possible to deduce from the known facts a plausible description of those early apartment houses, or tenements, which undoubtedly were characteristic of Tyre long before Strabo saw them. They probably rose above streets only a few feet wide, because space was at a premium. They were probably constructed at least partly of wood because cedar, oak, and fir forested Mount Lebanon, only a few miles inland on the eastern rim of a narrow plain, and because the Phoenicians are known to have been skilled carpenters: as shipwrights they were the best of their day. The climate was mild, and the sun bright, so it is likely that the flats had windows but no panes, for glass was imperfect and costly. They probably towered as high as six stories, for Carthage, which followed Tyre's example in most things, did have six-story houses.

If Tyre's skyscraper residences resembled those built not too much later in Rome and Ostia, their tenants cooked on charcoal braziers, drew their water from cisterns and wells or founts in the streets and squares, and used their glassless windows as plumbing. The apartment houses of Rome and its seaport suburb had strong foundations and well-built walls of brick at least up to the third floor; they probably rose much higher because contemporary Roman writers complained that they frequently collapsed, a tendency which undoubtedly motivated the Emperor Trajan's decree limiting building heights to 63 feet. Despite their failings, they were not entirely without amenities: some of the upper-floor apartments had their own private staircases, with treads of wood and risers of stone. But if they resisted collapse, they frequently burned, because charcoal braziers are not the safest of stoves.

Presumably, Tyre's apartment dwellers were no more pampered than those of Rome and Ostia, and neither were its pedestrians. Of the dangers the skyscrapers presented to passersby, the Roman satirist Juvenal wrote:

Look now at the other and various perils of the night. Consider the great height of the lofty roofs from which a tile may crack down on your skull and how often from those windows cracked and chipped pots crash down, leaving a mark on the pavement or damaging it with their heavy weight. You ought to be blamed for negligence and for being careless of sudden accidents, if you go out to dine at night in Rome without making a will. The passer-by at night has as many chances of death as there are windows where the tenants are still awake. You may well hope and utter this modest prayer that these windows will pour down on you no more than the contents of a large-sized basin.

What the people who lived in Tyre's apartment houses looked like must remain a matter of conjecture, for they left behind little or nothing of sculpture and painting to memorialize themselves, but they probably differed little in appearance from their Carthaginian descendants, who were slender of build, and whose males —except for the priests—sported beards and wore long straight woolen robes, usually beltless; if the Tyrians resembled their descendants in sanitary behavior as well, they were clean, for the Carthaginians used bodyscrapers, which were buried with them.

Religion and trade dominated Phoenician life, as they later dominated Carthaginian life. Alone among the peoples who spoke Semitic languages, the Phoenicians were sailors, who became the boldest explorers and later the wealthiest merchants of the Mediterranean—until their offspring, the Carthaginians, surpassed them in both exploration and trade.

The Phoenicians had to take to the sea. Their long, narrow homeland was bounded on the east by the lofty Lebanon mountains which looked to the Mediterranean on the west across a few miles of plain whose shepherds could not, despite the soil's richness, feed the population. The forests of Mount Lebanon, however, offered the best of timber for shipbuilding; Phoenicia boasted good harbors, and its cities were sited at the crossroads of the caravan routes by which silks and spices came from the Asian hinterland. They had another great resource—and an incentive to foreign trade—in the murex, a small sea snail which then abounded on Mediterranean shores. When the snail shell was crushed and its contents exposed to the sun in a vat excavated in rock, the product was a rich dye that varied in hue from scarlet to deep purple, depending on the period of exposure.

It is to be hoped that early anti-air pollution laws required the dyeworks to be situated downwind, for they stank. But the industry was highly profitable: the dye, which was known as Tyrian royal purple, because Tyre was credited with its discovery, was widely exported and became an early status symbol; St. Luke, for example, needed to say no more in his Gospel to describe a member of the affluent society than to mention a "certain rich man, which was clothed in purple and fine linen." Phoenicia acquired its very name from the dye, for the Greek word for crimson or purple is *phoinix*; the name, however, is all that remains to remind us of the murex, for, overexploited like many a later status symbol, it long since has disappeared from the Mediterranean.

Harbors, timber, geography, and a prized dye would not be enough in themselves to have made the Phoenicians explorers, for in the beginning ships were small and frail, sails were inefficient, there were no compasses, and the Phoenicians knew nothing of the hazards to navigation in the western Mediterranean. But they had courage and skills.

As early as the twelfth century B.C. they were sailing to the less civilized and sparsely settled lands of North Africa, southern Spain (called Tarshish in the Old Testament), Sicily, and the other Mediterranean islands, to sell their tools and weapons, their textiles, timber, glassware and trinkets, and their purple dye, in exchange for gold, silver, tin, iron, and lead.

They were good at it. Isaiah called Tyre a city "whose merchants were princes, whose traders were honored of the earth," but the competing Greeks were less flattering and Homer referred to the Phoenicians as "men famed for their ships, greedy knaves bringing countless trinkets in their black ships."

"Their black ships" survive only in Egyptian and Assyrian murals and reliefs, and it is impossible to do more than hazard an intelligent guess at their length and beam, their draft and tonnage, their rigging and speed. But it is likely that those ancient freighters—the "round ships"—were at least 50 feet long, with a vertical mast forward of amidships carrying a square sail and possibly jibs. A carved horse's head topped the stem, and the sternpost rose vertically; the craft was steered by two heavy oars pivoted on each side near the stern, and the master navigated by the stars and by landmarks. In such craft, Phoenician seamen employed by the Pharaoh Necho, Herodotus records, circumnavigated Africa about 600 B.C., taking three years to complete the voyage because they had to pause annually to plant and grow food. About a century and a half later, in similar ships, one party of Carthaginians sailed halfway down West Africa's coast and another rounded the coast of Spain and France to Britain, looking for new markets and for an efficient method of shipping home the tin of Cornwall.

The ships had to be good, and Herodotus, describing the expedition of Xerxes against Athens in 480 B.C., asserts that the Phoenicians furnished the best vessels: M. Pierre Cintas, the distinguished French archaeologist and authority on Carthage, believes that one and perhaps the major reason for Phoenician superiority was that the Phoenicians solved the problem of making watertight hulls by using pitch for caulking seams. Ezekiel appears to confirm this hypothesis by including caulkers among the skilled artisans of Tyre.

Unlike the neighboring Hebrews, who were a pastoral people, the Tyrians counted a wide variety of skilled artisans: when Hiram, King of Tyre (979–946 B.C.) helped King Solomon build his temple in Jerusalem, he sent not only cedar, cypress, and pine from Mount Lebanon, but architects, carpenters, and builders, and workers in stone and metal. It was a generous and neighborly gesture, for in religion the Phoenicians and the Hebrews differed vastly: the Phoenician faith, which at least in its earlier years involved the sacrifice of infants to Moloch, had a whole pantheon of cruel and licentious gods which horrified the fiercely monotheistic Hebrew prophets.

However powerful the gods, however deft the artisans, Tyre, like its offspring Carthage, depended largely for its wealth, even its livelihood, on overseas trade. So Tyre early developed a powerful navy, but Tyre and all Phoenicia had commercial, not political, objectives; the navy was meant to prevent competition and protect shipping against pirates who flourished in the Mediterranean from antiquity, as Thucydides points out, wherever commerce and coastal cities flourished.

Despite their strength at sea, Tyre and the other tiny kingdoms of Phoenicia were helpless against the aggressors surrounding them, and would have been even had they formed a strongly knit confederation. Egypt, Assyria, Babylon, Persia, and Macedonia had armies and resources far too great to be resisted by the Phoenician city-states, and in succession conquered the Phoenician kingdoms—with one significant exception. In the war with Babylon, Tyre successfully fought off a thirteen-year siege (585–572 B.C.) after every other Phoenician kingdom had surrendered, and during Phoenicia's nearly forty-years-long Chaldean-Babylonian captivity, Tyre alone maintained its independence. That proud memory inspired the Carthaginians in their defiance of the Roman ultimatum centuries later, in 149 B.C.

But even defeat did not necessarily mean humiliation and destruction. The successive conquerors of the Phoenician kingdoms valued seafaring skills and invariably granted the vanquished cities favored status. Usually land powers without navies, the victors welcomed the Tyrian fleet among their military resources and treated the Tyrians more like allies than like subjects. When Persia's King Cambyses conquered Egypt in 525 B.C., for example, Tyre became Persia's vassal, but grittily refused to furnish a convoy for the king's projected campaign against Carthage, and got away with her defiance. The episode foreshadows Carthage's reaction at the end of the Roman cold war, and a later event in Tyrian history sheds even more light on the character and behavior of the Phoenician people of Tyre and Carthage.

Tyre was still Persia's vassal in 332 B.C., when Alexander the Great led his Macedonian army southward through Phoenicia to Egypt to bar the Persian fleet from Phoenician harbors and to take over the Phoenician warships for his own use. Under his ultimatums, city after city opened its gates to him, and even Tyre sent envoys to him to say "Tyre has decided to accept Alexander's orders." The decision was hardly a firm one, however, in the light of what followed.

Alexander, who claimed he could trace his ancestry back to Hercules, informed the Tyrians "that he proposed to come to Tyre to sacrifice to Hercules" since Tyre encompassed "the most ancient temple of Hercules of which there is any record." But the Tyrians rebuffed the proposal as sacrilegious and politically dangerous; indeed, they were prepared to fight. Arrival of a Carthaginian delegation to help celebrate Melkart's annual festival had helped to stiffen Tyre's back: they promised that if it came to a siege, their navy would bring in men and supplies, and they urged Tyre to resist.

When Alexander got wind of the change of mind, he raged at Tyre's envoys: "You indeed, relying on your situation, because you live on an island, despise this army of foot-soldiers, but I will soon show you that you are on the mainland. Therefore I want you to know that I will either enter your city or besiege it."

Alexander had judged the Tyrians rightly. Like the Carthaginians, they held a strong natural position. Again like the Carthaginians, they had powerful fortifications; in addition, they had a navy and two harbors to serve it. Alexander initially had no fleet. The Tyrians could afford to be tough and scornful of Alexander's infantry: with Carthage's help, they could not lose, even to Alexander.

But it took months for word of Tyre's peril to reach Carthage, and it would have taken months more for a rescue convoy to arrive: if help was sent, it arrived too late, for Alexander wasted no time. He demolished the old section of the city, which was on the mainland, to obtain material for a broad mole out to the island, and when he had bridged the strait, he erected towers and sited engines of war at the mole's island end. The Tyrians responded with pots of flaming naphtha and sulphur, among other exotic weapons, and sent fire ships to wreck the towers and damage the mole. Alexander's engineers doggedly repaired the mole and rebuilt the towers. The battle raged for months. Eventually, having realized the need for a fleet, and having acquired

14

hundreds of ships by the surrender of Sidon, Rhodes, and many other city-states and having ingeniously placed battering rams on rafts, Alexander beat his way past the city's walls. The Tyrians resisted tenaciously, hurling stones and whatever else came to hand from the roofs of their skyscraper tenements. Alexander's troops slaughtered 8,000 Tyrians, executed 2,000 more, and sold 30,000 into slavery. The siege had cost Alexander seven months, a heavy price for a conqueror who had only thirty-three years for his lifetime. Though it ended in disaster, it was Tyre's finest hour.

The character and behavior of the Carthaginians were strongly influenced by the mother city's heritage and tradition. Throughout their centuries of existence, the Carthaginians, like the Tyrians, were the few against the many. Each—Tyre and Carthage —had to hire mercenaries for defense because its own population was too small to supply adequate armed forces. (Ezekiel, writing shortly after 600 B.C., noted that Tyre's troops included Persians and natives of five foreign cities.) Each produced bold explorers and each developed the trade by sea which brought the great wealth that proved irresistibly tempting to the empires of the day. Each loved peace, for commerce, not conquest, was the national goal and each used sea power chiefly to assist diplomacy in gaining national ends. Each had a measure of political deftness, which Tyre used to attain supremacy in Phoenicia, Carthage to build an empire. When they became vassals, they dowered their conquerors with skills and resources that usually won for them favored status. And each had a fanatical devotion to the religion of which Melkart was the dominant god; in defense of their gods and their cities, they displayed courage and tenacity that were remarkable.

The Phoenician character and the legacy of Tyre obviously explain many aspects of Carthaginian history.

III

CARTHAGE VS. GREECE

Long before Rome emerged from the obscurity that was all a small city-state on the hills above the Tiber merited, Carthage was growing in wealth and power. When Alexander was besieging Tyre, in 332 B.C., Carthage was the capital of an empire that stretched along North Africa's coast from the Greek colony of Cyrene on the east to and beyond the Strait of Gibraltar on the west. She had possessions in Spain that extended from her trading posts on the Mediterranean to Cadiz on the Atlantic coast. She occupied the west of Sicily, the coasts of Sardinia, and at least portions of every other large Mediterranean island. With Tyre's defeat, Carthage became the leader of the Phoenician world—albeit ever loyal to the mother city.

The Carthaginians intuitively sensed the truth of the still-unwritten adage that "trade follows the flag." Her explorers had tirelessly sought out beaches on the Mediterranean shores to the west where ships could be hauled up easily, where water and food were available, and where nature provided defenses. Traders followed the explorers. But rarely, unless mining operations made it necessary, did they penetrate deeply into the hinterland. They were primarily interested in commerce, not colonization.

Yet colonization was inevitable, and with colonization came problems, even quite close to home. Some of the problems were of Carthage's making, a failing, it must be said, of which much later colonial empires were equally guilty. When Carthage was founded, North Africa was already inhabited—undoubtedly sparsely—by white races of uncertain origins who were far less advanced than the city-dwelling, sophisticated Phoenicians.

One of these races, the Libyans, we have already met briefly. The Carthaginians agreed to pay the Libyans ground rent for the site of the city and they continued to pay this rent during several centuries. Under Carthaginian rule, the Libyan peasants were free men, but their graves reveal their extreme poverty. They were second-class citizens, burdened by high taxes which in wartime reached 50 per cent of their produce. As early as 396 B.C. a peasant uprising among the Libyans seriously threatened the existence of Carthage. There is ample confirmation in other and later rebellions that Diodorus Siculus (writing of this period about 40 B.C.) did not exaggerate when he described the Libyans who joined the Greek invader, Agathocles, as hating "the Carthaginians with a special bitterness because of the weight of their overlordship." Moreover, they had reason enough to regret the liberty they had formerly enjoyed in their nomadic life which was still the right of the free Libyans outside the Carthaginian area.

To the west of Carthage, along the coast and inland, lived the Numidians, whose name has come down to us as "nomads," to designate a people without fixed habitation. In a number of independent tribes, they roamed the area of modern Algeria, and on the Mediterranean shore they had established two kingdoms. When they were friendly to Carthage, they furnished her with the cavalry that formed the major tactical strength of her army. But they did not always remain friendly, for reasons that will be explored later; they helped Rome to victory in the Second Punic War (218–201 B.C.) and in the ensuing cold war became one of the most serious threats to Carthage's independence— and life.

Carthage managed to alienate not only the indigenous peoples who might have served her well, but also folk of her own flesh

17

and blood. Other Phoenician port cities were smaller than Carthage and depended on her powerful navy for their defense. All these cities, Utica and Cadiz among them, paid a price for Carthaginian protection and the price appears to have been high. For example, Leptis, the easternmost city in the Carthaginian empire, had to pay Carthage a talent a day, a sum impossible to estimate accurately in modern terms because the talent varied: that of Athens weighed 83 pounds whereas elsewhere it was as low as 58 pounds. Neither is it known whether Leptis paid in gold or silver. In any case, the tribute was a large amount of money.

Despite the tensions within and without, Carthage flourished. In the Medjerda River valley, and on Cape Bon, wealthy Carthaginians lived like planters of the American South before the Civil War. The estates around their country houses produced all the food that the capital and its surrounding territory could eat. But Carthaginian prosperity depended on foreign trade and prosperity, to continue, requires expansion.

The Carthaginians were not alone in their need to expand. In the city-states of Greece, growing populations made increasingly difficult demands on the limited lands available for producing the wheat and the olives that fed them and the grapes that cheered them. The pressures sent emigrants forth to found new cities. Cumae, now in ruins on its rocky hill near Naples, began life in 750 B.C., a little more than sixty years after the Princess Elissa founded Carthage. Less than a score of years later, a party of Corinthians chose an ideal site on Sicily's eastern coast for what became the city of Syracuse.

The fields of Sicily were so fertile that they fed Greece and later Rome for centuries. The island enjoyed a strategic position for commerce—and for war. The Greeks and the Carthaginians competed in the export and import business. The Carthaginians

18

had cities and towns on the island's western end, the Greeks on its east. Their spheres of interest conflicted, making inevitable the long wars that raged over the island from the sixth century B.C. on.

Greek and Carthaginian spheres of interest already had clashed on the African continent itself. The only European colony of the time in Africa, Cyrene, which the Greeks founded in 631 B.C. on a site ten miles from the sea in what is now Cyrenaica, threatened to block Carthage's expansion eastward in the direction of Egypt. The two cities fought, at a date that history has forgotten, and finally agreed to a boundary much closer to Cyrene than to Carthage. In Sicily, the Carthaginians were less successful: a defeat at Himera, on the island's north coast, in 480 B.C., for example, restricted them to the island's western region.

Commercial rivalries aside, Carthage's wealth and power early motivated a variety of greedy imperialists. By the end of the sixth century B.C. Carthage already had become famed for her riches, envied for her profitable overseas trade, and feared for her navy. The Persian king Cambyses cast covetous eyes on her after he conquered Egypt and made Tyre his vassal, but his campaign against her apparently never got beyond the planning stage, thanks, as we have seen, to Tyre's bravery. A little more than a century later, in 415 B.C., Alcibiades, one of the generals in the Athenian expedition against Corinth's Sicilian colony of Syracuse in the Peloponnesian War, found Carthage irresistibly tempting. But Athens suffered so grievous a defeat at Syracuse that Sicily never became, as Plutarch puts it, "the ways and means . . . for his [Alcibiades's] greater war." Diodorus debatably imputes a similar dream to Alexander, almost a century later.

The first invader finally came out of Sicily in the form of a Greek soldier of fortune whose military and political strategy became the model for all later invasions of North Africa.

19

The invader was Agathocles, tyrannical ruler of Syracuse. He was born in 361 B.C. in a small Greek city on Sicily's northern coast. His father was a potter, and so was he for a few years. But "he left his wheel and the clay and the smoke and came to Syracuse as a young man," according to Polybius, to seek his fortune. Strong and handsome, he had little difficulty marrying a wealthy widow, whose fortune helped him to power by the time he was forty-four years old, he had become ruler of Syracuse and, shortly, of nearly all Grecian Sicily. In the rapidity and the circumstances of his climb to power, he had few equals; in his character and career, he resembled another, much later, tyrant, Adolf Hitler. Both were of obscure and humble origin, both practiced humble trades, both came to rule countries in which they had not been born. Both committed incredible crimes, and believed in and practiced mass slaughter. But the quality which most strikingly linked the ancient tyrant and his modern counterpart was the ability to succeed, for a time at least, with reckless and unorthodox military movements, epitomized by Danton's advice: "De l'audace, et encore de l'audace, et toujours de l'audace."

He demonstrated the audacity after his first clash with Carthage. For centuries, the ups and downs of war made the border between Carthaginian and Greek dominions in Sicily extremely fluid. Carthage did not seek to dominate the island politically, for her commercial interests were adequately served by her possessions on the western portion. Wars of conquest did not seem worth a tetradrachma, but to protect the seaports in the west and to maintain the balance of power in Sicily, Carthage's merchant-princes were ready to fight.

In 311 B.C. they fought against Agathocles, with Greek allies who feared the upstart would seize all of Sicily, and trounced him; Agathocles lost more than half his army. Agathocles retired behind the powerful defenses of Syracuse, and the Carthaginians, with bigger land forces, began a siege of the city while their greatly superior navy blockaded the entrances to both its harbors. It looked like the end of Agathocles.

But the potter's son understood the value of surprise and *l'audace*. The situation he confronted was this: Carthage's army surrounded Syracuse. Her fleet commanded the Mediterranean. At home she had only a few men under arms, but the Mediterranean was a hundred-mile-wide moat. She had nothing to fear. Agathocles proposed to advantage himself of Carthage's sense of security. His plan was to leave in Syracuse, under command of his brother, a garrison just adequate for the city's defense; to embark a few thousand of his bravest and best soldiers on sixty ships; to slip through the enemy blockade; to land on the Cape Bon peninsula and to attack Carthage itself as the best way to defend Syracuse.

It was preposterous, on the face of it. But of the manner in which Agathocles won political control of Syracuse, Diodorus has written: "Of all men who ever came to power, none acquired a greater kingdom with fewer resources." It is safe to say that no other general ever undertook a campaign with so little preparation and with such relatively scanty resources as Agathocles in his attack on Carthage.

But Agathocles knew that the Carthaginians had virtually no army at home, and that their civilians were accustomed to luxury and inexperienced in war. He believed—rightly, it proved—that he could count on help from the Libyans whom Carthage had oppressed and exploited. He counted too on surprise, for he kept his plans secret.

By attack, he calculated, he would compel Carthage to lift the siege of Syracuse and at the same time enable himself to strike Carthage at its heart, just as more than twenty centuries later General Robert E. Lee's Antietam and Gettysburg campaigns threatened Washington and forced the Army of the Potomac to leave Virginia.

Agathocles sailed. He ran the blockade. He landed his men on

21

the Cape Bon peninsula, about seventy miles by land from Carthage. He promptly burned his fleet so that his men could not consider retreat and flight. For years, he occupied Carthaginian territory, pillaging and devastating the countryside. He persuaded the Greeks of Cyrene to join him, then murdered their general to eliminate a rival in the top echelon of command. He won many victories.

But like Hitler he failed to estimate at its true value the power of the human spirit. The Carthaginian will to resist in defense of its capital city—and the Carthaginian superiority at sea—frustrated him: he never took Carthage. And like Hitler, Agathocles died in flames. Apparently suffering from cancer of the mouth, he was laid on a funeral pyre while still alive but speechless. Diodorus commented: "Agathocles had committed numerous and most varied acts of slaughter during his reign, and since to his cruelty towards his own people he added impiety towards the gods, the manner of his death was appropriate to his lawless life." *Sic semper tyrannis*.

Agathocles's invasion of Carthage—the first—demonstrated the value of Cape Bon for such a campaign and it pointed the way for future aggressors.

Another aggression was not long in coming. In 280 B.C., only thirty years after Agathocles's first defeat by the Carthaginians, another Greek, Pyrrhus of Epirus, invaded Italy to wage war on Rome, and the following year carried the fighting into Sicily. Even before he attacked the island, Carthage had recognized the threat that Pyrrhus represented, and had formed an alliance with Rome. In Sicily, Pyrrhus—a worthy successor to Alexander the Great—inflicted severe defeats on the Carthaginian armies, which retired behind the strong defenses of Lilybaeum (modern Marsala). Pyrrhus attacked for two months before abandoning the siege. Three years of war had netted him nothing. Another conqueror had failed to subjugate Carthage. As a prophet, however, Pyrrhus had more success. Gazing on the Sicilian shore as he left for Italy's mainland, he said: "My friends, what a wrestling-ring for Carthaginians and Romans we are leaving behind us."

IV

THE FIRST PUNIC WAR

The wrestling match began in 264 B.C., eight years after Pyrrhus had perished in battle. It was to last twenty-four years and to become what Polybius called "the longest, most continuous, and greatest war we know of." Its outcome transformed the political and military shape of the Mediterranean world. And though Pyrrhus had foreseen it, the two contestants, Carthage and Rome, were slower in perceiving that events were sowing the seeds of discord.

During centuries of Graeco-Carthaginian rivalry, Rome had stood aloof, an indifferent spectator of events outside Italy. Rome's economy was agricultural, her interests military: she cared little about Mediterranean trade. During those centuries, Rome had accumulated neighboring city-states as military allies, while Carthage was intent on accumulating wealth. Later, Rome developed her ground forces, ostensibly to form a military alliance of all the cities of the Italian peninsula, which was destined in reality to become a Roman empire in Italy. Carthage built up a navy to defend her far-flung maritime empire and her foreign commerce which made her the trading center for the western Mediterranean. Carthage's wars with the Greek cities in Sicily were usually defensive wars to maintain the balance of power on that island or to keep trespassers away from her possessions in western Sicily. It is therefore not surprising that among the first acts of the Roman Republic—after Rome had expelled her hated Etruscan kings—was, according to Polybius, the signing of a treaty of friendship with Carthage in 508 B.C. The treaty restricted both sides in their political, military, and commercial activities but its terms favored Carthaginian trade, and barred Roman commerce from certain areas. The Romans had no objections: for all they cared, the western Mediterranean might remain a Carthaginian lake.

A similar treaty was signed in 348 B.C., and Livy mentions a third, in 306, which continued and confirmed friendly relations between Rome and Carthage. Rome was still indifferent to commerce and Carthage had no designs on Italy. Within three decades they were allies, fighting Pyrrhus and pledged not to make a separate peace with him.

Sixteen years later, they were at each other's throat and, though of course they could not know it, involved in a duel to the death. Escalation of a trivial *casus belli* into a major war is nearly inevitable when a poor but powerful people, taught by experience, as the Romans had been, that war is a profitable venture, comes into conflict with a wealthy mercantile nation of reluctant warriors. To understand how and why these former allies became bitter enemies, a closer glance at events just before 264 is needed.

Between 270 and 265 B.C., Rome subjugated and made allies of all the cities in southern Italy. That ended Rome's indifference to foreign commerce on the Mediterranean, for among her new allies were wealthy Greek mercantile cities of that region. Reggio (Rhegium), now a Roman ally, looked across the Strait of Messina to the strongly fortified one-time Greek city of Messina (Messana) which for many years had been in the hands of brigands who had murdered the males and enslaved the women and children. These men had been mercenaries from Campania in central Italy who had deserted Syracuse, their employer. Plundering their neighbors in Sicily, they made a good living and terrified the adjacent cities by calling themselves Mamertines—"sons of Mars." King Hiero of Syracuse decided to destroy them and led an expedition to take Messina. Thereupon a minority of the "sons of Mars" invited Carthage to aid them against Syracuse, an invitation which Carthage gladly accepted. But, alas for peace, the majority of the Mamertines sent a delegation to the Roman Senate to request that Rome rescue their now endangered fellow Italians. So Messina became a potential meeting place for Syracuse, Carthage, and Rome.

Carthage apparently got there first. The Roman Senate, reluctant to risk war with Carthage, shifted the responsibility to the Assembly of the Roman people, which made the mercenaries Roman allies. Down the peninsula with his legions marched Appius Claudius, one of the consuls for that year. He had orders to aid Rome's ally in Sicily. A small squadron of the minuscule Roman navy preceded him.

So the primary, immediate cause of the terrible First Punic War was a cry for help from a band of scoundrels. But some other pretext for war might have had the same consequence of Rome's arrival at both sides of the strategically and commercially important Strait of Messina. At any rate, neither Rome nor Carthage planned the First Punic War. Chance brought it to pass and chance continued to determine its development.

The First Punic War started with a skirmish, and, oddly, a peace conference. The few Roman ships clashed with a task force of Carthaginian vessels, presumably in the Strait of Messina, and the North African professionals overwhelmed the amateurs from the Tiber.

Leading from strength, and following the Carthaginian principle that it was better to talk than to fight, the Carthaginian commander Hanno proposed a conference to settle the dispute. As an earnest of good faith, he returned the captured triremes and their crews to Appius Claudius. Hanno felt confident that an agreement would be favorable to Carthage: his forces occupied Messina, and his powerful fleet stood guard. The waters between Scylla and Charybdis, with their rushing tides and treacherous winds off the mountains, were often too much even for skilled navigators; the Roman landlubbers would never get across, and almost certainly would not try to.

On the Italian side, at Reggio, Appius Claudius had an army bigger and better than that of the Carthaginians, but a navy hopelessly outclassed in size and skill. The Romans had the soldiers, the Carthaginians had the sailors; if the Romans wanted to get to Messina they would have to cross the strait in whatever small craft they could round up. Sea power faced land power, and in Reggio, Hanno faced Appius Claudius across a conference table. He began, no doubt, by reminding Claudius that "in urging him to agree to peace," as Dio Cassius recorded, he spoke from strength, not weakness. Presumably Claudius remained unimpressed, for Hanno began to talk tougher. He threatened Claudius with dire consequences of any aggression in Sicily, saying that he marveled "how the Romans could venture to cross over into Sicily, inasmuch as the Carthaginians had control of the seas; for it was obvious to all that if they did not maintain friendly relations, the Romans would not dare even to wash their hands in the sea."

Claudius still was not impressed. Before he left Rome, the Senate had ordered him "to cross to Messina" and he intended to obey orders. He too could rattle the saber with the arrogance befitting a Roman consul. He replied: "We advise you not to teach us to busy ourselves with the ways of the sea. We Romans are pupils who always outdistance our teachers. . . . If you Carthaginians compel us to learn naval warfare, you will soon see that the pupils have become superior to their teachers."

The conference broke up. Hanno returned to Messina, relying on the Carthaginian fleet to keep the Roman army from crossing the strait. He relied too much. Under cover of darkness, Claudius dispatched his army to Sicily in scores of small craft, besieged Messina, and forced Hanno to abandon the citadel. The Carthaginians thereupon crucified Hanno, "thinking him," Polybius reports, "guilty of a lack both of judgment and of courage in abandoning the citadel." Crucifixion was an occupational hazard in the top echelons of the Carthaginian army and navy.

As the struggle in Sicily continued, Carthage and Syracuse forgot their hundreds of years of warfare and joined forces against the Romans. But the alliance was short-lived. The Romans defeated them both and Syracuse sued for peace and offered to become an ally of Rome. The Romans gladly accepted.

The war had started with limited objectives, but it soon was being fought for higher stakes, because Rome and Carthage both realized that Sicily "would furnish to the side that conquered it a safe base for operations against the other party." The prize for the winner in the First Punic War would be Sicily and the command of the western Mediterranean.

Despite Hanno's misadventure the war went well for Carthage at first. Her fleet effectively blockaded Sicilian ports, and the Roman army went hungry, while Carthage reinforced and supplied her own army at will. Only in the fifth year of the conflict did Rome, recognizing the importance of sea power, decide to build a navy large enough to challenge Carthage in the element she dominated. The Romans went about it methodically. Using a captured enemy warship as a model, they built a fleet and trained its crews ashore, on rowers' benches. A hundred quinquiremes and twenty triremes and their crews were ready in a remarkably short time.

The admiral, Gnaeus Cornelius Scipio, one of the two consuls, sailed for Messina with seventeen ships to set up a supply base; the rest of the fleet was to join him when the base had been established. About what happened next, stories conflict, but Gnaeus—an amateur admiral—and his fleet were captured on the island of Lipara, about forty miles northwest of Messina. Polybius says that twenty Carthaginian ships, arriving opportunely, "shut up Gnaeus in the harbor. When day dawned the Roman crews hastily took refuge on land, and Gnaeus, falling into a state of terror and being unable to do anything, finally surrendered to the enemy."

As a permanent reminder of his failure, the Romans bestowed a fourth name on Gnaeus—and his descendants. It was Asina. Whether it meant blockhead, or merely referred to the fear of water which is attributed to the *asina*, or she-ass, is not clear. In any case, Hanno may have suffered the lesser punishment.

The general commanding the Roman legions in Sicily was the Consul Duilius. No sailor he. But when he heard of his colleague's misadventure, he turned his army over to the military tribunes who were his staff officers and took command of the Roman fleet. Ignorant of the techniques of naval warfare, Duilius knew he was ignorant, and that his crews could not match the enemy in the complex maneuver of ramming which characterized sea combat at the time. So Duilius had a gangway constructed near the bow of each of his ships, and set it on a pivot.

When Roman and Carthaginian ships met in the battle of Mylae, off Sicily's northern coast, in 260 B.C., the gangways swung out, and boarding detachments of Roman soldiers made short work of Carthage's outnumbered and inferior mercenaries. "The battle having become just like a fight on land," in Polybius's words, the Carthaginians "finally gave way and took to flight, terror-stricken by this novel experience." They had lost fifty ships.

In recognition of his victory, Rome gave Duilius a triumph, and a little extra: an after-dark escort of torch-bearers and flute players.

But one battle does not necessarily win a war, and Rome was not yet mistress of the seas. As the conflict dragged on, naval domination shifted back and forth. In truth, the Romans had a long way to go to become great sailors, and lost more men to the inexperience of their admirals than to the enemy. Storms proved a deadlier foe than the Carthaginians: One, in 255 B.C., destroyed all but eighty of a Roman fleet of 364 ships, "covering the shore with corpses and wreckage," according to Polybius. He adds: "History tells of no greater catastrophe at sea taking place at one time." In all, storms during the war sank seven hundred Roman warships and drowned two hundred thousand men.

Centuries later the Romans still had much to learn about the sea, and Vegetius, writing his *Epitome of Military Affairs* in the fourth century A.D., felt it necessary to warn them that while certain months are entirely suitable for naval operations, some others are questionable and still others absolutely impracticable. Navigation is safe from the end of May to the middle of September. But no admiral in his right mind would put to sea from mid-November to mid-March, for days are short, and in the long nights clouds and fog hide the stars. Then, only a merchantman in search of profit would have the temerity to sail the Mediterranean.

Agathocles had proved that the Mediterranean was no impassable moat around the Carthaginian citadel. In 256 B.C., in one of the periods when the Romans did have the upper hand at sea, they followed Agathocles's example and strategy, landing an expeditionary force on the Cape Bon peninsula at Clupea, about seventy-five miles from Carthage. Led by Marcus Atilius Regulus, the Roman troops swept over the peninsula, devastating farms and estates, and defeating Carthaginian armies sent against them. The resentful Numidians happily joined the fray, rebelling against Carthaginian domination in open warfare.

Other baleful Carthaginian chickens came home to roost too. The Carthaginians, like other commercial-minded nations after them, neglected their military establishment in time of peace. They selected their military leaders, as we shall see, too often for political or family influence. They failed to support their generals and admirals in time of war.

So for the second time, Carthage was in a desperate situation.

Atilius Regulus offered to negotiate and the Carthaginians accepted gladly—until the Roman general arrogantly demanded unconditional surrender.

The Carthaginians reacted as they always did when the odds against them were so enormous that further resistance seemed insane: they rose in their wrath. "The attitude of the Carthaginian Senate on hearing the Roman general's proposals," wrote Polybius, "was, although they had almost abandoned all hope of safety, yet one of such manly dignity that rather than submit to anything ignoble or unworthy of their past they were willing to suffer anything and to face every exertion and every extremity."

Forthwith, they displayed energy and intelligence that, exercised earlier, might have saved them much of their travail. As sometimes happens when a people displays intelligence and energy, the Carthaginians had a stroke of luck, for which they no doubt thanked their gods. In the moment of their deepest desperation, a recruiting officer for their army of mercenaries returned from Greece with a tough Spartan, Xanthippus, and with "a considerable number of soldiers." Xanthippus looked things over and laconically announced that "the Carthaginians owed their defeat not to the Romans but to themselves, through the inexperience of their generals."

Carthage bestowed command on Xanthippus and he reformed training, discipline, and tactics. Then he defeated and captured Atilius Regulus and saved the city. A few Roman survivors escaped to Clupea, and were rescued in a small-scale Dunkirk. Xanthippus had proved that even mercenaries, hitherto inferior troops, could beat the Roman legions when properly led.

The war impoverished and exhausted both sides, and disasters had virtually swept the Romans from the sea. Rome's treasury was empty. But in 243 B.C., Rome determined to build another fleet "as the only way of bringing the war to a favorable conclusion," and Roman citizens patriotically provided funds for two hundred quinquiremes.

In battle near the Aegates Islands, off Sicily's west coast, the Romans sank fifty Carthaginian ships, and captured seventy, with their crews. The Carthaginian admiral escaped, but his fellow citizens put him to death on the cross. The last great Carthaginian fleet was gone. Carthage lost Sicily and Rome acquired a tribute-paying, subject province. To both victor and vanquished, the First Punic War taught an unforgettable lesson of the influence of sea power on history. It was then that according to Polybius the Romans "not only gained the courage to aim at universal dominion, but executed their purpose." Roman imperialism, having completed its domination within the Italian peninsula, had begun its march throughout the world surrounding the inland sea.

V

REVOLT OF THE

MERCENARIES AND THE

UNNUMBERED PUNIC WAR

Weary from their long campaigns and costly battles, the Carthaginian army's veteran mercenaries returned from Sicily to Carthage demanding their back pay and their discharges. But twenty-four years of war had emptied Carthage's treasury, which was trying to find the cash to make the initial payment on Rome's war indemnity, a staggering 3,200 talents, payable in ten annual installments. The twenty thousand mercenaries, who came from Libya, Numidia, Spain, Gaul, Greece, and Sardinia, rebelled. Eager to throw off the Carthaginian yoke, thousands of Libyans and Numidians and their women joined the mutineers: the Libyans alone soon totaled 70,000.

The rebels spoke a dozen different tongues, and had great difficulty communicating with each other, but they were united by hatred of Carthage, and a runaway Roman slave, Spendius, and a Libyan, Matho, whipped them into a fighting force. The Carthaginians, Polybius writes, "had chiefly themselves to thank for all these grievous mischances. During the late Punic War they had thought themselves reasonably justified in making their government of the Libyans very harsh. They had exacted from the peasantry half of their crops, and had doubled the taxation of the townsmen. . . . They had applauded and honored not those governors who treated the people with gentleness and humanity, but those who procured for Carthage the largest amount of supplies and stores and used the country people most harshly. . . . The consequence was that the male population required no incitement to revolt."

The Revolt of the Mercenaries, also known to historians as the Truceless or Inexpiable War, erupted in 241 B.C. It lasted three years and four months, and before it was over, even Carthage's sister cities, Utica and Bizerte, deserted her to fight beside the Libyans, Numidians, and mercenaries. For Carthage, it was a life-or-death struggle: Polybius writes that "in this war the Carthaginians encountered many great perils and finally were in danger of losing not only their territory, but their own liberty and the soil of their native city." It was fought, apparently, with extreme ferocity, for Polybius comments that it "far excelled all wars we know of in cruelty and defiance of principle."

When the rebellion started, Carthage, which maintained no standing army, had only the citizen soldiers of what she called the Sacred Band to defend her against an enemy army that numbered as many as a hundred thousand men. The Sacred Band, recruited from the aristocracy, comprised fifteen hundred infantry and a thousand cavalry, formed the bodyguard of the commanding general and served as a *corps d'élite* for ceremonial occasions and probably as a school for future staff and general officers. It must have been also a nucleus for assembling and training citizens as soldiers when the city itself was threatened. Around the Sacred Band, another Carthaginian general named Hanno mobilized a force of undetermined size, but though Hanno was a competent organizer and administrator, he could not win battles. So Carthage called on Hamilcar Barca to command a second army of ten thousand men; a gifted general, Hamilcar Barca led his troops to victory in their first battle.

What happened next was characteristic of the Carthaginians,

who had alienated their neighbors the Libyans and the Numidians, their own mercenary army, and even their sister cities. A difficult people! After Hamilcar Barca's victory, Hamilcar and Hanno engaged in a bitter feud. "They quarreled so seriously," writes Polybius, "that this difference caused them not only to neglect many opportunities of striking a blow at the enemy, but to afford many such to the latter."

It was characteristic of the Romans and the Sicilian Greeks, too, that during the rebellion they sent a limited amount of aid to the Carthaginians, whom they had been fighting so short a while before. Obviously mutiny must not be encouraged, no matter where. It might give ideas. . . .

Carthage's Senate found a way to end the Hamilcar-Hanno feud. It authorized the men of each army to vote for one of the quarrelsome generals as the future commander of both. The soldiers chose Hamilcar. Hanno retired—temporarily.

Some time earlier, "a Numidian of high rank and full of martial spirit," as Polybius puts it, Naravas by name, had joined Hamilcar with two thousand Numidian horse. He had left his Numidian countrymen, who were allied with the mercenaries, because of "his family's attachment to the Carthaginians and his own admiration for Hamilcar." Naravas's cavalry helped Hamilcar's army to cut off supplies for the enemy's main force which was actually besieging Carthage. Starvation caused the besiegers to lift the siege, a reversal of the usual roles in warfare.

Hamilcar's superb generalship then maneuvered an enemy force of 40,000 men into a position where he surrounded them with a trench and palisade. Reduced to cannibalism, Spendius and nine other leaders in the rebellion (Matho with the rest of the mercenaries was at the base in Tunis less than ten miles from Carthage) went as envoys to Hamilcar to ask for terms. He agreed to let all others go free if "the Carthaginians might choose from the enemy any ten they wished." When the envoys agreed, Hamilcar announced that they were the ten men he chose.

The enemy troops, ignorant of the treaty, took up their arms and Hamilcar "cut them all to pieces."

The Carthaginians crucified Spendius in the sight of both the armies below the walls of Tunis. In retaliation, Matho, in command of Tunis, crucified Hamilcar's second in command, whom he had taken prisoner. Thereupon Hanno returned to the army, evidently a chastened man, and the reconciled leaders pursued Matho to Leptis, where his army was destroyed and Matho himself taken prisoner. And Polybius writes that "the last scene in it [the rebellion] was a triumphal procession of the young men leading Matho through the town and inflicting on him all kinds of torture."

But such victories as Carthage's are worth little more than defeat. The nation had been bled white by twenty-seven years of war and its countryside lay devastated. Carthage was helpless, and Rome saw an opportunity to take advantage of the situation without risking the life of a single man.

The opportunity centered on Sardinia, the large island west of Italy, and only a little smaller than Sicily. It had been Phoenician territory since the ninth century B.C. and its mines, its timber, its war-loving manpower for hire, and its position on the trade routes made it of great strategic and economic value to Carthage. It is a mystery that it was not included in the spoils of victory after Rome won the First Punic War. It is no mystery, however, that the Romans refused to take over Sardinia during the rebellion. The mercenaries there, after killing all the Carthaginians they could find on the island, invited Rome to step in. Rome declined, just as she declined to accept Utica's offer to surrender to her: a budding empire did not encourage violations of law and order, or defections of allies, even if they were the enemy's.

But the Romans were not blind to Sardinia's importance, for, as Polybius notes, "the Romans . . . from the moment they concerned themselves with the sea, began to entertain designs on Sardinia."

Carthage's prostration in victory made the time ripe for turning designs into actuality. We do not know whether Roman agents fishing in troubled waters were responsible for another invitation to Rome, from mercenaries who had deserted to Rome from Sardinia, to take over the island. In any event, the invitation was given, and promptly accepted. Rome landed an army of occupation. Carthage, naturally, objected.

Calling Carthage's verbal protests "preparations" for war, but perfectly well aware that Carthage was "in every respect ill-fitted at this moment to resume hostilities with Rome," as Polybius puts it, Rome's Senate declared war. It was an act of infamy—obscured by later acts of infamy—that foreshadowed Rome's strategy of terror, blackmail, and conquest without bloodshed.

The Carthaginians, "yielding to circumstances . . . not only gave up Sardinia," Polybius records, "but agreed to pay a further sum of 1,200 talents to the Romans to avoid going to war for the present."

Even Polybius, who was pro-Roman, was shocked. Rome's declaration of war, which was made in 238 B.C., had, he said, "no reasonable pretext or cause" and he commented scathingly that "the Carthaginians, contrary to all justice, and merely because the occasion permitted it, were forced to evacuate Sardinia and pay the indemnity."

Thus ended, before it began, the Punic War that remained un-numbered. Carthage never forgot or forgave the injustice it represented, and her resentment nourished the seeds of the Second Punic War.

VI

THE SECOND PUNIC WAR

Few nations had suffered the troubles that beset Carthage and survived, and in 238 B.C. it did not seem that Carthage could survive. Her people were destitute, her fields and forests were devastated, her commerce and industry were disrupted. She could not defend herself or her territories. But she had one priceless possession, Hamilcar Barca, who had emerged in the First Punic War as the one outstanding Carthaginian general and who later had won the Truceless War.

Hamilcar Barca was virtually unique among Carthaginians in that he had a surname to distinguish him from other Hamilcars, and the surname was most appropriate, for Barca means "lightning." It described his most notable military attribute.

Hamilcar indulged in no idle dreams of revenge. He had, instead, a plan for a Carthaginian renascence, and it involved the exploitation of Spain. Hitherto, Carthage had not penetrated Spain much beyond its coasts. But Hamilcar reasoned that in Spain he would find the men, the mineral wealth, the trade, and the strategic position to restore his homeland materially, morally, and militarily. With a small army, and with his young son Hannibal, Hamilcar sailed to Spain in 237 B.C. Polybius records that before he died in battle against "one of the most warlike and powerful tribes" in 229 B.C., "he reduced many Iberian [Spanish] tribes to obedience either by force of arms or by diplomacy."

Hamilcar's son-in-law Hasdrubal, who succeeded him in command of the army, continued the work of developing the new province, and founded New Carthage, the modern Cartagena, as the capital of this land of promise. But a Celtic assassin cut short his life and his rule of Spain in 221. Hamilcar's son Hannibal was now twenty-eight, and although he had not seen Carthage since he was ten, his reputation for character and prowess was so great there that Carthage appointed him commanding general in Spain.

Hannibal's rise to power resembles that of Alexander the Great. Each, still young, inherited a strong army from his father. Each learned the principles of leadership, military and political strategy, and tactics from a great father who did not live to finish his work. Neither Philip of Macedon nor Hamilcar Barca of Carthage had reason for disappointment in his son.

In the first three years of his service as commander in Spain, Hannibal came into conflict with Roman interests there. It is not surprising, for when he was nine years old, his father had led him to an altar to swear "never to be the friend of the Romans." Rome sent a delegation to Carthage. "Surrender Hannibal to us or we declare war," the delegation threatened. "Do as you please," the Carthaginians replied. "War, then," said the Romans, and war it was. The year was 218 B.C.

Rome's strategy for this new war was based on two facts: She had plenty of manpower, and the Mediterranean was virtually her own preserve, in which no enemy fleet presented a danger. So she proposed to send one expedition to Spain, and another to invade North Africa.

But to Rome's astonishment, Hannibal moved first, with daring and total surprise. Unlike most Carthaginian generals, Hannibal was a professional soldier and owed his command to recognized ability rather than to politics. He was expert in strategy and tactics, for he had studied the campaigns of Alexander the Great, he had been instructed by his father, and he had learned by experience in his own campaigns in Spain. In addition, he had acute political sense.

Since Rome commanded the sea, he would attack her overland: he would profit by necessity, he hoped, and along the way stir Rome's bitter enemies, the Gallic tribes living north of the Po River, to join his invading army and to provide a supply base, since the Romans would surely cut his line of communications to Spain.

So, from his base in Cartagena, Hannibal led "about 90,000 foot and 12,000 horse," plus a number of elephants intended to terrify the enemy, up through southern Spain, across the Pyrenees, across the Rhone River, and across the Alps into Italy. The mountains, the rivers, the weather, and hostile native forces all resisted his advance, but in five months he marched eight hundred miles, at a price. Just how high a price is a point on which the old historians differ. Polybius says Hannibal reached Italy with scarcely 20,000 infantry and 6,000 cavalry, and gives no figures for the elephants, either at the start or the finish. Appian puts the figures at 48,000 infantry, 8,000 cavalry, and 15 of the 37 elephants with which Appian believes he set out.

It may well be that allies recruited en route account for the discrepancies, for Hannibal never lost sight of his political objective while pursuing his military objective. He was intent on gaining support from nations already hostile to Rome, and on detaching subject peoples in Italy from Roman domination. To that end, he released captive soldiers who came from cities allied to Rome, explaining that "he was not come to fight with the Italians, but with the Romans for the freedom of Italy." Actually, though, he had relatively little success at this, among the Italians, at least, for Rome treated her vassal neighbors in far more enlightened fashion than Carthage had treated the Libyans and Numidians.

Militarily, however, Hannibal had vastly more success. His army was always inferior in numbers to the enemy's, but as Polybius explains, he had developed it to be "highly efficient and in the highest state of physical training." Hannibal's superb tactics on the battlefield, however, determined the victories he won. In the first major battle with the Romans he proved that point. On a bitter-cold, snowy night in late December, 218, the Consul Sempronius was camped with 40,000 infantry and 4,000 Gallic cavalry, south of the Po, near the Trebia River. Hannibal, on the other side of the Trebia, sent a band of Numidian cavalry to make a screaming predawn raid on the Roman camp. Angry, Sempronius took the bait; his army forded the Trebia in icy water nearly up to their shoulders. Hannibal's 40,000 men, of whom 10,000 were better-trained and more reliable horsemen than the 4,000 enemy cavalry, were in position. Sempronius, advancing without proper reconnaissance, did not detect a detachment of 2,000 picked men under Hannibal's brother Mago hidden behind a low ridge. Sempronius attacked but failed to dent Hannibal's line. The Carthaginian cavalry cleared the field of Rome's Gallic horsemen and charged the Roman flanks while Mago's men, effecting the complete surprise which was essential to the trap that Hannibal had set, sprang on Sempronius and his army from the rear, and completed the encirclement. Only 10,000 Romans escaped from this battle which Hannibal all his life considered his most brilliant tactical success.

The next battle, however, proved a greater victory in terms of prisoners and booty. April, 217, had arrived and so had Hannibal and his army in a position hidden in the hills above and parallel to the road along the shore of Lake Trasimene about seventy miles north of Rome. The Roman Consul Flaminius had to take that road with his 40,000 men. In history's greatest ambush, Hannibal charged the long marching column and Flaminius was unable to form a line of battle. When the attack ended, Flaminius and 15,000 of his men were dead and Hannibal had 15,000 prisoners, who were held for ransom or sold into slavery if they were

Romans, or set free and allowed to go home if they were merely allies of the Romans.

After that battle Hannibal marched south along the Adriatic coast. His men needed rest, re-equipment with captured weapons, and more training. It was a year of little fighting, for the Roman general, Fabius the Delayer, avoided battle with Hannibal.

But in 216 Rome decided to launch an offensive against Hannibal, who had not had more than 35,000 men at Trasimene and had certainly received not more than 5,000 recruits from the few friendly people in Italy. Rome had mobilized an army of 85,000. Word reached Rome that Hannibal had captured a supply depot at Cannae, a few miles from the Adriatic, about two hundred miles southeast of Rome. The eight legions under the two consuls with cavalry and supporting troops, nearly 90,000 men according to Polybius, met Hannibal on the plain near Cannae on August 2 or 3, 216. The tactical skill Hannibal displayed in defeating this greatly superior force is unparalleled in military history. It has become the classic example of encirclement on both flanks with a decisive cavalry charge on the Roman rear. Polybius records 70,000 Roman infantry killed and 10,000 captured, and nearly 9,000 cavalry killed. Carthaginian casualties numbered 5,700.

Hannibal's victories were monuments to his military genius, but they owed at least something to the Romans themselves and to their practice of making their annually elected consuls their commanding generals and admirals in war.

Surrounded by his staff and his division commanders, Hannibal debated the next step. Everyone except Hannibal's chief of cavalry, Maharbal, recommended a night's rest for the exhausted troops. Maharbal urged immediate pursuit, and offered to ride ahead with his cavalry while Hannibal followed with the infantry. "In five days you shall banquet in the Capital," he promised. Hannibal rejected the advice and the disappointed Maharbal blurted out: "In very truth the gods bestow not on the same man all their gifts; you know how to gain a victory, Hannibal, you know not how to use one."

Maharbal's accusation is moot. Hannibal did not immediately march on Rome, and Livy concludes his description of the episode with the observation: "that day's delay is generally believed to have saved the City and the empire." But Hannibal lacked a siege train and his army was too small to storm the City's walls— good reasons for not pressing on at the time. Five years later, he did march to Rome's walls, but he did not besiege the city, for he understood the dictum of the world's oldest military treatise, written by Sun Tzu three hundred years before Hannibal: "If you lay siege to a town, you will exhaust your strength. If the campaign is protracted, the resources of the state will not be equal to the strain." Hannibal comprehended the problems of logistics, as many of his critics did not. Instead of besieging Rome, Hannibal, aware of his inability to take the city by assault, adopted an indirect strategy in a war of attrition.

Hannibal's younger brother Mago, who had already distinguished himself at the Trebia, carried to Carthage the news of the victory at Cannae. The Carthaginian Senate convened to receive his report. Mago began by emptying a bushel of gold signet rings of a kind worn only by the most distinguished Romans: they had been taken from the dead on the battlefield. He proudly gave the number of enemy casualties. Then, having laid the groundwork, he told the Senate that supplies and money were needed at once to complete the conquest of Rome.

But Carthage's Senate, like many a senate which followed it, suffered from chronic disunity. It was divided now between Hannibal's supporters and a pro-Roman antiwar party whose members' prosperity was more important than victory. One of Hannibal's supporters in the Senate turned to Hanno, the leader of the opposition, and taunted: "Let us hear the language of a Roman senator in the senate-house of Carthage." Hanno obliged. Opposing the dispatch of supplies to Hannibal, he asked, "After all, what are those boasted advantages [of the victory at Cannae]? 'I have cut to pieces the army of the enemy,' says Hannibal. 'Send me troops.' What else would he ask if he had been defeated. 'I have taken two camps of the enemy, filled with plunder; send me grain and money.' What else would he ask if his own camp had been taken?"

Despite Hanno's deftness at irony, the Senate voted to send Hannibal the aid he requested. But Livy adds, "As usual in times of prosperity these orders were executed with indolence and remissness." The reinforcements never reached Hannibal.

But if Hannibal could not get them from home, he got them abroad, by dint of his triumphs. Capua, the wealthiest and most luxurious city in Italy and a center of industry, opened its gates to Hannibal a few months after Cannae—a serious blow to Rome's pride and prestige.

The next year, 215 b.c., Philip V of Macedon, across the Adriatic from Italy, allied himself to Carthage. The bandwagon accelerated. In 214, Syracuse rebelled against Rome to give Carthage still another ally and deprive Rome of a valuable naval base in Sicily.

In time Rome's superior power on land and sea ended these internal and external threats to her chances of defeating Carthage. Two years after breaking her alliance with Rome, Syracuse was recovered by Marcellus in command of a joint army and navy punitive expedition. Syracuse resisted desperately and repulsed successive assaults largely because of the inventive genius of her mathematician and scientist, Archimedes; his derricks at the walls along the waterfront dropped heavy lead missiles on the attacking ships or, still more alarming to the victims, they caught hold of the bows of the ships with massive claws which lifted them on end and suddenly let go. Archimedes contrived a precursor of napalm, using his catapults to hurl missiles of flaming pitch which fired the wooden ships. Treachery inside the walls, however, delivered Syracuse to Marcellus. He sacked the city and subjected it to stern military control.

Capua fared even worse. It had deserted Rome, and to discourage similar defections, Rome in 212 sent a strong force to besiege the city. Hannibal arrived by forced marches from Tarentum, a city he had occupied, but failed to dislodge the larger Roman armies in their well-defended siege works. But he had an idea: a march on Rome would force the besieging army to lift the siege. Only a detachment, however, followed him. And in Rome, while he remained for a few days before its walls, devastating the surrounding country and gathering booty, Hannibal created panic only among the women and children. The move on Rome proved futile. Capua was starved into surrender, its power elite executed, and its territory confiscated.

Philip V of Macedon failed to bring any effective aid to Hannibal because the Roman navy commanded the Adriatic. And in this fashion Rome had nothing more to fear from the consequences of her defeat at Cannae.

From the start of the Second Punic War, Rome had maintained a second front in Spain, which was essential to Hannibal as the base for his Italian operations and as a source of manpower. But after Hannibal's brother Hasdrubal—who bore the same name as their predecessor in command—had defeated two Roman armies in Spain, no Roman wanted the dubious honor of heading Rome's forces there. Then the twenty-four-year-old scion of a distinguished family stepped forward. In spite of his youth and the consequent legal barriers to office, he was appointed proconsul to command the Roman army in Spain. His name was Publius Cornelius Scipio, to which a few years later he would be able to add Africanus.

Within a year, Scipio captured Cartagena, Hannibal's Spanish headquarters. Scipio's considerate treatment of the Spaniards won them over to loyal support of his rule, and the realistic Hasdrubal quit the country with his army in 208 B.C. to go to his brother's aid in Italy.

To outwit Scipio, he left Spain by a northwest passage over the Pyrenees, heading for winter quarters in central France, where the friendly Gauls gladly aided him with men and supplies. He reached the Alps when the snow melted, took Hannibal's route over the mountains and crossed the Po River with additional Gallic recruits. Hannibal, who had wintered in 208-07 in the toe of the Italian boot and now was marching north to their reunion, reached Canusium, only a few miles from Cannae, and there he expected news from his brother. The news, when it came, was ghastly.

Hasdrubal had written a letter describing his route south along the Adriatic. He would meet Hannibal in Umbria, in central Italy, near that sea, and together they would march on Rome. The bearers of the message, four Gauls and two Numidians, journeyed safely through almost all of Italy, then fell into the hands of a Roman detachment near Tarentum. It was a fateful misfortune. When the Roman Consul Gaius Claudius Nero read the letter, he speedily joined forces with the other consular army under Marcus Livius and together they engaged and annihilated Hasdrubal's army near the Metaurus, a river flowing into the Adriatic northeast of Rome. Hasdrubal died in battle, and the Romans tossed his severed head into Hannibal's camp. The grim incident marked the turning point in the Second Punic War.

In the next two years, Scipio completed his conquest of Spain, and won a consulship as reward. He now proposed the long-postponed Roman invasion of Africa, which Hannibal had prevented in 218 by crossing the Alps into Italy. But Scipio's plan seemed too daring to Rome's elderly senators. The idea of an offensive appealed to them, provided Scipio attacked Hannibal in Italy, but to carry the war to the enemy in Africa would leave them undefended.

Not at all, Scipio replied. Hannibal brought the war to Italy thirteen years ago; he is still here. Agathocles and Regulus invaded Africa with consequences to Carthage that just missed being fatal. If I invade Africa I shall draw Hannibal after me. I shall not let him hold me back. I shall compel him to fight in his own land. Carthage will be the reward of victory, not the half-ruined strongholds of southeast Italy to which Hannibal has been forced to retire.

Hannibal's thirteen years in Italy had been frustrating and exasperating indeed for the Romans. One after another, Rome's generals had confronted him with everything in their favor—their armies were far larger than Hannibal's, they were better supplied and better armed, and they should have had better morale, for they were defending their homeland. They fought supported by well-fortified cities as pivots of maneuver, cities that Hannibal lacked the means to capture. Hannibal's outnumbered mercenaries and Gallic allies had to live off the country. Yet, by dint of Hannibal's military genius and his rare qualities of leadership, they had repeatedly beaten and outmaneuvered the Romans.

In a search as baffling to Rome as was Lincoln's quest for a general to outmatch Robert E. Lee, the Romans had sought a soldier with enough brains and character to crush Hannibal. They never found him, for Scipio found himself.

Despite Scipio's persuasiveness, Rome did not send him off to Africa with its blessing. In the face of Hannibal's presence in Italy, and despite the opposition of most Roman military experts, the Senate assigned Scipio to Sicily. It did give him permission to go to Africa—if he insisted—but it sat smugly confident that he would never get there, for the Senate refused him an army.

Scipio moved to Sicily in 205 B.C. While Hannibal awaited reinforcements that never came, Scipio trained an army of volunteers for Africa, collected transports, and built a fleet. In 204 he was ready, crossed the Mediterranean with 400 of the transports and 40 warships, and landed his expeditionary force near Carthage.

And where was the Carthaginians' vaunted navy? History does not say: in any event, it gave Scipio no trouble.

Scipio's campaign after landing need not detain us, except to note that the following year he decisively defeated a Carthaginian army and its allies under Hasdrubal, son of Gisgo. Scipio then divided his force, assigning the larger part, which he commanded, to devastate the country and seize its cities and towns; the smaller detachment he sent to besiege Utica, which he needed as a base of operations.

Today, Utica, or its site, is six miles inland, the silt-laden Medjerda having formed a delta around it. But in Scipio's time, Roman galleys, with a mere four-foot draft, could row right up to its sea wall.

By lashing two galleys together, Scipio was able to erect on the foundation that they provided a wooden tower higher than any in Utica's ramparts. From a platform atop the tower, catapults battered at the city's defenses.

Undoubtedly other pairs of galleys supported scaling ladder devices which Rome's navy had used earlier at the siege of Syracuse, and possibly even battering rams. Utica's walls suffered heavy damage. But the city did not sit passive under attack; it hurled stone projectiles at the galleys and scored telling hits.

Morale in Carthage meanwhile had sunk to a new low. Most of the army at home was gone. Many cities had surrendered. The ruling class was still divided—a chronic failing of Carthaginian character—and when a Carthaginian delegation went to Rome to ask for an armistice, it blamed the whole war on Hannibal. But the armistice ended and a peace treaty offered by Scipio came to naught.

For at this juncture, the Carthaginian Senate decided to recall Hannibal from Italy, where he was now in his sixteenth year. Simultaneously, it ordered the navy, which had been training all winter for such an operation, to take the offensive against the Roman fleet. The time was favorable. Scipio, expecting no trouble from the enemy's ships, had immobilized his own by using them in his siege of Utica. His army, except for the portion at Utica, was holed up in Tunis, twenty-three miles by road from the besieged port. If Carthage's fleet could accomplish its mission, Carthage would have a better chance of a favorable negotiated peace.

The high-walled naval base inside Carthage had screened the fleet which had managed to keep its preparations secret. When Scipio, standing on the high ridge on which Tunis was built, saw Carthage's fleet setting out in the direction of Utica, he was taken by surprise. He sent a messenger speeding off with orders to his fleet to improvise a rampart of four hundred transports around the fighting ships, and he gave his army the word to march to Utica.

Scipio probably reached Utica in about three hours. The rampart of merchantmen was only beginning to take shape. To form the barrier, which was to be four transports deep, each transport had to be towed into place and lashed to its neighbor. The wall was far from completion when Carthage's ships, having rounded Cape Carthage, hove in sight: not even a start had been made on laying a gangplank on the outer row of vessels, from which a thousand picked defenders could fight. Once again, Rome was depending on the courage of her soldiers to win victory at sea.

When the Carthaginian fleet reached the scene—having rowed or sailed eighteen miles—the Roman fleet lay vulnerable and virtually helpless. A bold admiral would have attacked at once. Livy comments that such an attack "would have been overpowering when everything was confused by the mass of men dashing about."

But the Carthaginians did not attack. Perhaps, if their crews had had to row all the way, they were exhausted. Perhaps, as Livy suggests, Carthaginian morale was too low as a result of the defeats Scipio had inflicted on their armies. In any case, they continued nine miles to the nearest Carthaginian town, now called

48

Porto Farina, northeast of Utica. They arrived at sunset. But they were up early next morning. Before sunrise, Carthage's fleet put to sea and drew up in battle formation, to await the Roman fleet, which was half its size.

The Romans did not come out. They could not. After hours of waiting, the Carthaginians moved forward to attack. Livy describes the ensuing action as not like a naval battle at all, but an attack by ships against a city's walls. In this instance the four-ship-deep ramparts must have interposed more than a hundred feet of wooden walls between the Carthaginian and Roman warships.

What an opportunity to shoot fire-tipped missiles at the enemy's conglomeration of wooden merchant vessels and galleys, or to drop fire pots from the ends of long poles—a device long in use. But the Carthaginians, great sailors though they had been, succeeded only in throwing heavy boathooks on some of the enemy galleys; grappling, they backed water to break up the front line of transports.

Even so, they did well. Sometimes the Romans could not cut the lashings between their ships fast enough, and a single Carthaginian warship would move astern towing a pair of them. About sixty transports thus were towed away by the stern to Carthage, but Rome's fleet had by no means been wiped out. The Carthaginians knew how to plan a surprise attack, but they did not know how to utilize their advantage to the full.

It was a victory of sorts, however, and Carthage was overjoyed, for it was the first victory over the Romans in many a year. Livy reports that the Carthaginians were aware that "the Roman fleet had narrowly escaped destruction and would have been destroyed if the admirals of their own ships had not loitered, and if Scipio had not come to its aid in the nick of time." But there is no record that the Carthaginian navy attempted to follow up its minor success with a major one.

When Hannibal received his orders to return to Carthage, he remarked, according to Livy: "It is no longer obscurely but openly that I am being recalled by men who, in forbidding the sending of reinforcements and money, were long ago trying to drag me back. The conqueror of Hannibal is therefore not the Roman people, so often cut to pieces and put to flight, but the Carthaginian Senate by carping and envy."

And Appian, describing the same episode, writes that Hannibal "lamented the perfidious and ungrateful conduct of the Carthaginians toward their generals, of which he had had long experience."

History records few greater ironies than the emergence, from a population of peace-loving traders, of a strategist and tactician such as Hannibal, almost unequaled in any age. Polybius, loyal friend to Scipio, says: "No one can withhold admiration for Hannibal's generalship, courage and power in the field" who thinks of his sixteen years of constant warfare in Italy, with a mercenary army of many nationalities and races, which he held together

under his personal command, like a good ship's captain [keeping] such a large army free from sedition towards him or among themselves. . . . The ability of their commander forced men so radically different to give ear to a single word of command and yield obedience to a single will. And this he did, not under simple conditions but under very complicated ones, the gale of fortune blowing often strongly to their favor and at other times against them. Therefore we cannot but justly admire Hannibal in these respects.

With these loyal veterans, or rather with the survivors, who probably numbered not more than 15,000, Hannibal, obeying orders, sailed for Africa in the summer of 203 B.C. His arrival at Leptis raised Carthaginian morale; his countrymen, regaining the will to resist the Romans, broke the truce and ended the peace negotiations. Then Scipio, who had occupied Tunis, adopted an indirect strategy. He marched away from Carthage up the Med-jerda valley to destroy the main sources of the city's food. He wanted also to draw closer to Masinissa whose 4,000 cavalry and 6,000 infantry might mean the difference between victory and defeat if Hannibal pursued him. The Carthaginian Senate directed Hannibal to march from Hadrumetum, where he had wintered, to engage the enemy.

Thus far Scipio's strategy had worked. The 40,000 men of his war-hardened legions, which have been called "the best which had ever fought for the cause of Rome," encamped close to the battlefield Scipio had chosen, an open plain which offered an ideal site for his superior force of cavalry (4,000 Numidian and 2,700 Roman horse). The exact location of the battlefield is un-known, but it is called Zama, although it was nearer to a town named Naragara. Hannibal arrived with an army that also totaled about 40,000 men, but was sadly inferior in quality to Scipio's. Its cavalry consisted of 2,000 newly recruited, untrained, and un-reliable Numidians. Hannibal, however, had eighty elephants.

Hannibal asked for a conference to discuss peace terms. Scipio consented. The two met. The exact date is unknown, but it al-most certainly was in the spring of 202. The confrontation of two of the world's most notable soldiers was rare and dramatic. Each had left his army several miles to his rear. Their escorts stood on the alert some distance away, leaving Scipio and Hanni-bal, each with his interpreter, together. Scipio's terms proved un-acceptable to Hannibal, and Livy records that "without making peace they returned from the conference to their armies, reporting that words had been of no avail. . . . Whether Rome or Carthage should give laws to the nations they would know the next day before nightfall. For not Africa, they said, or Italy, but the whole world would be the reward of victory."

Next day, they fought the battle of Zama. Hannibal's front-line elephants, which he had counted on to terrify the enemy, failed to do their duty. The din of Roman shouts and trumpets panicked those on the left as they approached Scipio's front ranks. They turned tail and charged into Hannibal's Numidian cavalry, demoralizing it. With the elephants went Hannibal's one hope of breaking through the Roman front. And with the demoralization of his cavalry went his chance of charging the Roman flanks and rear, as he had done at Cannae.

There were a few moments during the day-long struggle when Hannibal's veterans came close to victory. But the Numidian and Roman cavalry, returning just in time from the pursuit of the Carthaginian horse, fell upon the flanks and rear of Hannibal's best troops. When evening and defeat arrived together, Hannibal's losses were 20,000 killed and wounded and about 20,000 taken prisoner; Roman historians, probably understating the figures, report only 2,000 dead from their army. Hannibal rode back to Hadrumetum with a small escort.

Hannibal had met defeat for the first time, and Scipio had laid the foundation for the future Roman empire. As Polybius put it some forty years later: "The Carthaginians [were] fighting for their own safety and the dominion of Africa and the Romans for the empire of the world."

Scipio's political objective was not, however, total destruction. When—most chivalrously for that epoch—he did not demand the surrender of Hannibal himself, he made it clear that he believed reconciliation with a weakened but autonomous Carthage was desirable. He intended that the war should result in a just and more enduring peace by requiring Carthage to abstain from war as an instrument of policy. The terms he proposed for a treaty were that Carthage should give up all territorial possessions outside her own boundaries; pay an indemnity of ten thousand talents of silver in annual installments over fifty years; surrender all elephants and warships with the exception of ten triremes, presumably for defense against pirates; not "make war at all on any nation outside Africa and on no nation in Africa without consulting Rome"; and become a friend and ally of Rome.

With Hannibal back in Carthage, some diehards in the Carthaginian Senate proposed rejection of the terms and continuance of the war. But Hannibal counseled acceptance, calling the terms lenient, as they were indeed under the circumstances. The peace treaty, signed in 201, demonstrated that Rome's statesmen were not arrogantly seeking revenge for Hannibal's sixteen years of occupation of their homeland, but rather wanted to prevent future wars.

Hannibal lived another nineteen years. At first, he devoted his energy, intelligence, and courage to the reform of Carthage's government, and his struggle against corruption and injustice endeared him to the people. But it made bitter enemies for him among many of the rich and dishonest politicians. To rid themselves of him, they sent word to Rome in 195 that Hannibal was plotting with King Antiochus of Syria to make war on Rome. When a Roman commission arrived to investigate, Hannibal fled by sea to Tyre and then to King Antiochus in Ephesus.

Rome relentlessly pursued him to frustrate his efforts to gain allies for Carthage and restore its greatness. Finally, his last friend, King Prusias of Bithynia, was ready to yield to Roman pressure and deliver him into Rome's hands. Hannibal poisoned himself; thus died the man who had been Rome's most feared and most formidable enemy. At last the Romans could breathe freely, for Carthage joined her conquerors in the desire for peaceful coexistence. Content to build and expand her trade, she might never have fought again had it not been for a disappointed lover who was to become the instrument of her eventual destruction.

VII

COLD WAR

IN A ROMAN TOGA

The disappointed lover was a prince of magnificent physique and great personal beauty. His name was Masinissa, and he was born in 238 B.C., a year of both good and evil portent for Carthage. It was the year that Hamilcar Barca crushed the rebellious mercenaries and Libyans, a portent for good. It was the year that Rome, taking advantage of Carthage's exhaustion, stripped her of Sardinia and her other possessions and imposed a second war indemnity, a portent for evil. It was the year that Hamilcar began rebuilding Carthage's economy and her military power in Spain, another portent for good. But none of those portents was so pregnant for Carthage as the birth of Masinissa, and it was a portent for evil.

Masinissa's father was king of the Massylians, a Numidian tribe dwelling along the Mediterranean in what is now western Tunisia and eastern Algeria. They were the Numidian people closest to Carthage, but in Masinissa's youth they were not the largest or the most powerful tribe: they were surpassed by the Massaesylians who lived farther west, on the approaches to the Strait of Gibraltar, and who were ruled by a king named Syphax. The rivalry and warfare between the Massylians and the Massaesylians were age-old.

The young Masinissa was, unwittingly, to heighten the enmity. Sent to Carthage to be educated, he met Sophonisba, daughter of the most aristocratic family in Carthage. She was, says Dio Cassius, "conspicuous for beauty, had received an excellent literary and musical education, and was clever, ingratiating, and so charming that the mere sight of her, or even the sound of her voice, sufficed to vanquish everyone, even the most indifferent."

Masinissa fell in love with Sophonisba, and she with him. Numidian royalty and Carthaginian aristocracy often intermarried, and Sophonisba's father, Hasdrubal, son of Gisgo, happily betrothed his daughter to the handsome prince. Then Hasdrubal and Masinissa left Carthage to fight the Romans in Spain, for this was the time in the Second Punic War when Hannibal was threatening the very existence of Rome itself, and Rome was retaliating by attacking Hannibal's Spanish base.

Unhappily for the young lovers, King Syphax of the Massaesylians also had been smitten by Sophonisba, and Syphax did not take defeat easily in either love or war. When he learned of Sophonisba's betrothal to the prince of the Massylians, he led his army against Carthage. Lacking an army itself, the Carthaginian Senate acted in desperation: without consulting Hasdrubal or Masinissa, it gave Sophonisba in marriage to Syphax.

In Syphax, Carthage gained a powerful ally, but in Masinissa it gained an eventually even more powerful enemy. He was through with Carthage forever. Though he still was serving with Hasdrubal, he secretly made an alliance with Scipio, who was in command in Spain. But, as Appian tells it, "Hasdrubal detected it, and although he was grieved at the outrage put upon the young man and his daughter, nevertheless thought that it would be an advantage to his country to make away with Masinissa. So when the latter returned from Spain to Africa at the death of his father, he sent a cavalry escort with him and told them to put him to death secretly in whatever way they could."

Masinissa, however, learned of the plot and frustrated it, proving himself to be, as Polybius described him, "one of the best and most fortunate men of our time."

Now—in the last years of the Hannibalic War—Masinissa turned against Carthage his 20,000-man cavalry, well-trained, hard-hitting, and fast-moving, and as elusive as Mosby's men in the American Civil War.

By his own example, Masinissa had accustomed his men to a frugal existence. He taught them to endure hunger and hardship, and their mounts seldom if ever tasted grain, and survived on little water. Effectively, they waged guerrilla war on the combined armies of Carthage and Syphax, which far outnumbered Masinissa's cavalry, but which, as Appian says, "marched with wagons and a great load of luggage and luxuries. On the other hand, Masinissa was an example in every toil and hardship, and had only cavalry, no pack animals and no provisions. Thus he was able easily to retreat, to attack, and to take refuge in strongholds. Even when he was overtaken, he often divided his forces so that they might scatter as best they could, concealing himself with a handful until they should all come together again, by day or by night, at an appointed rendezvous. Once he was one of three who lay concealed in a cave around which his enemies were encamped. . . . Thus his enemies never could make a regular assault on him, but were always warding off his attacks."

Baffled by these guerrilla tactics, the Carthaginians and Syphax's Numidian forces failed to defeat Masinissa before Scipio invaded Africa in 204 B.C., and when the Romans did arrive, they and Masinissa together won a number of battles. In the last one before Hannibal's return to Africa, according to Appian, Masinissa and Syphax met in combat. Syphax's horse, wounded, threw him. Masinissa personally took Syphax prisoner and turned him over to Scipio. Thus speaks Appian, who delights in making a good story better. Building up Syphax's defeat and capture into a Homeric tale of single combat, which is probably apocryphal, was a temptation he could not resist. History ends Syphax's biography thus: Sent to Rome, Syphax "sickened of grief and died." With Rome's help, Masinissa added Syphax's kingdom to his possessions.

Sophonisba hastened to send word to Masinissa explaining that she had been forced to marry Syphax. "Masinissa accepted her explanations gladly and married her." Evidently, since Syphax still lived, kings needed no writ of divorce. But the marriage ended swiftly and tragically. Syphax triumphed in the end. Appian reports that he told Scipio: "Sophonisba, the daughter of Hasdrubal, with whom I fell in love to my hurt, is passionately attached to her country, and she is able to make everybody subservient to her wishes. She turned me away from your friendship to that of her own country, and plunged me from that state of good fortune into my present misery. I advise you—to beware of Sophonisba lest she draw Masinissa over to her designs, for it is not to be expected that this woman will ever espouse the Roman side, so strongly is she attached to her own country."

Scipio took Syphax's advice. He ordered Masinissa to deliver Sophonisba to him. Masinissa demurred. Scipio "ordered him more sharply not to try to possess himself by force of any of the spoils of victory," says Appian, "but to ask for her after she was delivered up and obtain her if he could."

Masinissa had to choose between Sophonisba and Rome. Unhappily, he chose Rome. Accompanied by a Roman detachment, he set out for his palace at Cirta, now Constantine in Algeria, where Sophonisba awaited him; eluding his guards, he secretly rode ahead to talk to his beloved. He carried a vial of poison and gave her a choice: to take the poison or to become a Roman captive. "Without another word he rode away. She showed the cup to her nurse, told her not to weep for her, since she died gloriously, and drank the poison." Masinissa's last gift to his wife of a few days was "a royal funeral."

The tragedy, which Corneille dramatized in Sophonisbe, evokes one of the "ifs" with which history is replete. If Masinissa had been allowed to keep Sophonisba as his wife, his hatred of Carthage—which had been born of his frustrated love for the girl—might have mellowed: with the help of those Carthaginians who favored reconciliation with him and hoped for Carthage's union with Numidia, the rift might have been healed and the old association perhaps re-established. Such an outcome could have changed the course of history, for it was Masinissa's aid to Scipio at the battle of Zama that weighed the balance against Hannibal and won for Scipio the surname Africanus.

If some men are born great, if some achieve greatness, and if some have greatness thrust upon them, Masinissa must be considered thrice great. As a king's son, he was born to greatness. By intelligence, leadership, and physical prowess, he transformed Numidia—with the help of Roman legions—from two warring states and an agglomeration of nomad principalities and sheikdoms into a united, civilized land of farms, towns, and cities, thus achieving greatness. And the Romans, recognizing his qualities and rewarding him for his loyalty, thrust greatness upon him, hailing him as King of Numidia. They had never bestowed similar honor on any foreigner.

Masinissa had earned it. He continued to earn it, in payment for the military aid he had received from Rome in unifying Numidia. In Livy's annals of the year 190 when Masinissa was only forty-eight years old, the Roman historian writes that Masinissa was "by far the richest of the kings of Africa and equal, whether in majesty or in power, to any king whatsoever in the whole world." For the next forty years the seemingly indestructible and ageless monarch served as the instrument by which Rome, ever maintaining an innocent countenance, waged a cold war on Carthage in furtherance of world revolution.

The revolution, in progress throughout much of the epoch with which this book deals, marked the end of the era of the city-state. Moving slowly through the Mediterranean world, it swept hundreds of city-states into larger units which were eventually to fall under the dominion of the universal Roman empire. That empire had been conceived in the unnumbered, unfought Punic War, when Rome discovered that the mere threat of force could win a bloodless victory. The empire was born in the Second Punic War, when the conquest of Spain and the Mediterranean islands and Roman victories to the east completed the transformation of the little land power which had been confined to the Italian peninsula into the mistress of the sea.

But after the signing of the treaty of 201 B.C., Carthage, like modern Germany, prospered in defeat, and if she recognized the revolution for what it was, she gave no sign. She found that the new relationship with Rome—in which she lay at Rome's mercy —interfered not at all with her principal preoccupation, the amassing of new wealth. Her commerce, industry, and agriculture thrived and her fat-living city-dwellers and wealthy estate owners gave little thought to changing the *status quo*. Prosperity, however, was doubtless unevenly divided and there were in Carthage serious internal difficulties, typical of the city-state at all times. Plato in *The Republic*, written more than two hundred years earlier, pointed out the consequences of the incredible internal class warfare that existed for centuries in the oligarchic cities of his time. Such a state, wrote Plato, "was not one but two States, the one of the poor, the other of the rich men; and they are living on the same spot and always conspiring against one another." Now Carthage, which never really lost the city-state outlook in governing her loosely knit empire, did not escape these class differences. But these internal clashes were obviously compounded by the problems of foreign relations in Carthage before the Third Punic War. Appian describes it thus:

There was a Roman party, a democratic party, and a party which favored Masinissa. Each had leaders of eminent reputation and bravery. Hanno the Great was the leader of the Romanizing fac-

tion; Hannibal, surnamed the Starling [of course not the Hannibal of the Second Punic War]; and Hamilcar, surnamed the Samnite, and Carthalo, of the democrats."

Of these Carthaginians named here, only Carthalo appears again in Appian's history. The party headed by Hannibal the Starling argued for reconciliation with Masinissa and union with Numidia; the party of the people advocated independence of both Rome and Numidia. But the dominant majority, headed by the moneyed aristocracy, sought only to further friendship with the Romans and appease them when necessary.

Neither Rome nor Masinissa had equally pacific intentions, although only Masinissa demonstrated his overtly. Just how soon Masinissa began harassing Carthage after the treaty of 201 B.C. had been signed is not clear, but the time could not have been long, for Livy writes that when a Roman commission arrived in Carthage in 195 B.C., the Carthaginians assumed it had come to settle their differences with the Numidian king. In any event, by 193 B.C., Masinissa—again according to Livy—had ravaged the Carthaginian coast, exacted tribute from certain of Carthage's dependent cities, and seized all the Carthaginian trading posts along the Mediterranean west of the Carthaginian boundry. Carthage appealed to Rome.

Again and again, during the next forty years, Carthage appealed to Rome. Each time Rome sent arbitrators, and each time the arbitrators carried instructions "to favor Masinissa as much as they could," says Appian, or "as before to help Masinissa secretly. They artfully confirmed Masinissa in the possession of what he had taken before."

The truth was that Rome was waging a cold war, and encouraging a satellite to wage a small hot one.

Even Polybius, friendly to Rome, does not try to defend Rome's duplicity. He wrote:

In Africa Masinissa, seeing the numbers of the cities founded on

*the coast of the Lesser Syrtis [the gulf in the angle between the
eastern coast of Tunis and the northern coast of Libya] and the
fertility of the country [around these cities of which Leptis was
the most important] which they call Emporia, and casting
envious eyes on the abundant revenue derived from this district,
had tried not many years before the time I am dealing with, to
wrest it from Carthage. He easily made himself master of the
open country as he could command it, owing to the Carthaginians, who had always been poor soldiers, having latterly become
completely enervated in consequence of the long peace. He could
not, however, get hold of the towns, as they were carefully
guarded by the Carthaginians. Both parties [i.e., the Carthaginians
and Numidians] appealed to the Senate about their differences, and
numerous embassies had come from both on the subject,* BUT THE
CARTHAGINIANS ALWAYS CAME OFF SECOND BEST AT ROME, NOT BE-
CAUSE THEY HAD NOT RIGHT ON THEIR SIDE BUT BECAUSE THE JUDGES
WERE CONVINCED THAT IT WAS IN THEIR OWN INTEREST TO DECIDE
AGAINST THEM. [Emphasis mine. D. A.]

The disputed territory rightly belonged, Polybius concedes,
to Carthage, but the Carthaginians "not only lost the country
and the towns in it, but had to pay in addition five hundred
talents for the intervening revenue of it since the dispute orig-
inated."

Carthage had sunk to the depths of degradation under the
weight of its obsession with wealth. "At Carthage," Polybius observed, "nothing which results in profit is regarded as disgraceful;
at Rome, nothing is considered more so than to accept bribes
and seek gain from improper channels." Carthage's mothers did
not raise their boys to be soldiers, but to be traders, manufac-
turers, or slave-owning farmers: foreign mercenaries could do the
fighting, and plenty of them could be recruited from underde-
veloped countries where lower standards of living prevailed
than even those in the Roman rural regions.

Until the treaty of 201 B.C. had reduced Carthage's fleet to ten triremes—hardly enough to serve as a coast guard—Carthage had maintained her navy chiefly in the furtherance of trade, i.e., the pursuit of wealth. For Carthage, even war was, to paraphrase Clausewitz, a continuation of business by other means. Carthage had fought the Greek city-states in Sicily and in Cyrene in North Africa because the Greeks competed in world trade or threatened their trade routes and rivaled the Carthaginians at sea. They endangered Carthage's prosperity, and for Carthage, that— and virtually that alone—justified war. Otherwise, Carthage preferred peace—at almost any price, except when an enemy attacked Carthage itself. In a world shared by Romans—and thus far there always have been Romans of one kind or another to share it— the price can be too high.

For the Rome of Carthage's years of degradation, war embodied the essence of policy. Rome suffered progressively from a disease which, to coin a word from the Greek *polemos*, for war, might be called polemomania: she had a psychopathic attraction to war. In furtherance of conquest and territorial expansion, the Roman Senate had no trouble persuading voters to support war, for the spoils of conflict reduced taxes. But more than the desire for material gain lay behind Roman policy. Rome lusted for world dominion and the lust grew as obsessive as Carthage's concern with wealth. And as one of her own historians, Florus, wrote, Rome "scattered the flames of war over the whole world."

But a Rome can become too rapacious, and a Carthage will suffer only so much. The first faint sign that a breaking point did exist appeared in 154 B.C. Curiously, it resulted from a development in Spain, where two thousand years later the Spanish Civil War served as curtain-raiser for World War II.

In the first centuries of Roman expansionism, Rome had proved herself an enlightened colonizer. The Roman Republic comprised an Italian federation under the rule of law, and even lesser members of the federation enjoyed treatment generous enough to keep them loyal—as Hannibal had discovered in his efforts to win Italian allies. Rome's approach was, for its time, revolutionary. Carthage, by contrast, had dominated, exploited, and even oppressed her neighboring cities and territories to the point where Sardinia and Utica defected and the Libyans and Numidians rebelled.

But as Rome grew in power, she became oppressive too. And in 154 the Lusitanians (in modern Portugal), joined soon by their neighbors, the Celtiberians (in modern Spain), rose violently against Roman rule. Hard-pressed, the Romans called on Masinissa for help. He sent cavalry and elephants—how many is not stated—commanded by a son, whose name is not recorded. In a severe defeat suffered by the Romans, Masinissa's son, it is surmised, took refuge in a Celtiberian town which was the objective of Masinissa's rescue operation to Spain. Appian has nothing further to say about Masinissa's march or the rescue of his son. We may assume he succeeded, however, because in another part of his history he reports that in the following year, 153, the Roman army was joined by "300 Numidian horse, sent to him by Masinissa, and ten elephants" which seem to have been the remnants of the previous year's expedition.

Masinissa's absence from North Africa in 154 gave the Carthaginian party, which Appian calls "democratic," a god-given opportunity. Carthalo, unquestionably a member of the Barcid faction, saw clearly that "while the Romans were at war with the Celtiberians, and Masinissa was marching to the aid of his son, who was surrounded by other Spanish forces," was the time for action, even if it violated the peace treaty of 201. Carthalo, who was the commander of auxiliaries, i.e., a force of mercenaries, and about whom we know nothing else, attacked "the subjects of Masinissa who were encamped on disputed territory." These auxiliaries were perhaps the force of Numidians, mentioned by Livy, under Arcobarzanes, the grandson of Syphax, come to avenge the death of his grandfather in Roman captivity and to aid

Carthage against Masinissa, the hereditary enemy of his family. Perhaps the pro-Roman appeasement party within Carthage got the upper hand and countermanded Carthalo's orders. In any event, Carthalo's attack failed. Its significance lay not in its failure, however, but in the fact that for the first time since the treaty of 201 B.C. had been signed, Carthaginians had dared to resort to arms without Roman permission.

The immediate aftermath was to be expected. Masinissa, returning from Spain to his kingdom in the fall of 154 B.C., decided to teach the Carthaginians a lesson, to discourage them from trying again. What better way than to take from them the fertile Great Plains, in the Medjerda River valley, not much more than seventy-five miles southwest of Carthage? It was land he long had coveted. He claimed also, and apparently seized, "the country belonging to fifty towns, which is called Tysca"—probably Dougga, which, not far from the Great Plains, became a Roman town whose ruins are well preserved.

Carthage had never won an argument before, but she tried again and appealed to Rome to arbitrate. This time the Romans modified their pro-Masinissa tactics ever so slightly. Instead of sending arbitrators forthwith, as they promised, "they delayed," according to Appian, "until they conjectured that the Carthaginian interests were almost entirely ruined."

The commission did not reach the site of the dispute until the following year, 153 B.C. It was headed by a man named Cato.

VIII

CATO COMES TO CARTHAGE

Marcus Porcius Cato, who had been born a plebeian, was Rome's most honored citizen. He had served his country with great distinction as consul, senator, censor, and soldier: he had begun his military career fighting Hannibal in the Second Punic War and in 194 had become a general rewarded with a triumph for a military victory in Spain. There was in him such strength of body and mind that in whatever rank he had been born, Livy wrote, "he would have been likely to win fortune for himself." In 153 B.C. he was eighty-one but, as Livy added, "Old age, which subdues all things, could not break his great spirit." Or his vigor: he fathered a son at the age of eighty.

He was also a conservative, self-righteous ascetic whose miserliness was the jest of Rome: he sold his slaves when they became too old to work in the fields, so that he would not have to feed them, and Plutarch records that Cato boasted "he left in Spain even the horse which had carried him through his consular campaign, that he might not tax the city with the cost of its transportation." Money-loving Carthage was not the kind of place for which Cato would have had much sympathy under any circumstances.

As Cato's ship sailed along Carthage's powerfully fortified sea front on an April morning and approached the entrance to the port, he must have gazed long and hard at the capital of Rome's age-old rival. Merchant vessels filled the harbor, at the far end of which, behind a circular wall, stood the navy yard. What was behind the navy yard wall did not worry Cato. He knew, through Rome's intelligence services, that the Carthaginians had honored the peace treaty of 201 B.C. restricting them to an anti-pirate fleet of ten ships. A sea wall with four-story-high towers (at 200-foot intervals) guarded the city's shoreline, and behind it the city climbed the partial amphitheater of hills crowned by temples. Six-story buildings crowded together along three streets leading up to the Byrsa, the formidable acropolis surrounded by inner fortifications. The streets bustled with people bent on the daily tasks of international trade that made Carthage wealthy: evidence of prosperity and of luxury abounded everywhere—and Cato loathed the soft life and easy livers.

So did Masinissa. He and Cato, though one had been born a prince and the other a commoner, were kindred souls. Masinissa too fathered a son in old age—at eighty-six; until his death at ninety he could mount his horse unaided and spend all day on its unsaddled back. Livy records that Masinissa's "habit was to eat and enjoy plain dry bread without a relish"; and Polybius has written that "a little before his death he defeated the Carthaginians—and next day he was seen in front of his tent eating a dirty piece of bread." Polybius adds that "to those who expressed their surprise [he] said he did it . . ." Unfortunately the rest of the fragment does not survive and Masinissa's explanation is unknown.

Cato had come to Carthage to arbitrate between the Carthaginians and Masinissa, and Cato's sympathies undoubtedly lay with the Numidian. Carthage never yet had won such an argument but this time the Romans must have taken Carthage's complaints more seriously than usual: otherwise they would not have sent their most distinguished citizen, and an octogenarian at that. Perhaps Rome's continuing difficulties in Spain had something to do with it.

But if Cato had any intention of even pretending fairness to

Carthage, the Carthaginians gave him no opportunity. Their back-bones stiffened by the news from Spain, the Carthaginian negotia-tors refused to negotiate anything but Masinissa's violations of the peace treaty of 201.

Enraged, Cato sailed for home. But more than rage moti-vated his next step. Genuine fear enhanced his hatred of Carthage. Cato was an authority on military affairs and had written the first Roman military treatise, now lost. He saw in prosperous Car-thage a potentially dangerous enemy. He remembered that Car-thage had offered to pay the entire balance of the crushing war indemnity imposed in 201 B.C. only ten years later. Rome had refused the lump sum but Cato knew that the last installment would be paid in 152 B.C., the year following his abortive mis-sion. Carthage's treasury would have a surplus for the hire of mercenaries if the city was of a mind to resist further aggression. In Carthalo's raid, and in the Carthaginian refusal to cooperate with the delegation that Cato had headed, Cato detected evi-dence that Carthage might soon be of such mind.

Cato's homeward voyage, probably favored by winds and tides, took only three days. Even that must have seemed long to the impatient old man. His mood and that of his companions is described by Appian, who wrote that while they were in Car-thage, they had "carefully observed the country; they saw how diligently it was cultivated, and what valuable resources it pos-sessed. They entered the city too and saw how greatly it had increased in power and population since its overthrow by Scipio not long before [202 B.C.]; and when they returned to Rome they declared that Carthage was to them an object of appre-hension rather than of jealousy, a great and hostile city, near at hand and growing thus easily."

Cato reported promptly to the Senate. As usual, in spite of his eighty-one years, he spoke eloquently and convincingly.

As he talked, Cato contrived—according to Plutarch—"to drop some Libyan figs in the Senate as he shook out the folds in his toga, and then, as the senators admired their size and beauty, said that the country where they grew was only three days' sail from Rome." It was a sharp reminder that the threat to Rome of which he was warning lay close at hand. He declared that Rome's liberty would never be secure while Carthage existed and, his gray eyes flashing, he concluded with a resounding cry: "*Delenda est Carthago*"—"Carthage must be wiped out."

More than two centuries later, Pliny the Elder commented tongue in cheek on the story of the figs:

What is the most astonishing thing in this story? A stroke of genius or mere chance? The swiftness of the journey or virile forcefulness? It seems to me that nothing could be more wonderful than that that powerful city which for 120 years had competed with Rome for world domination was finally overthrown on the evidence of a single piece of fruit. It achieved what neither Trebbia nor Trasimene, neither Cannae, the grave of Rome's proud name, neither the Carthaginians in their well-fortified camp three miles from Rome nor Hannibal himself riding his horse to the Colline gate could accomplish. So much nearer to Rome did Cato move Carthage by means of a fig.

Cato did not, however, move P. Cornelius Scipio Nasica, who had been consul two years before. He argued that "Carthage ought to be spared so that Roman discipline, which was already relaxing, might be preserved through fear of her."

Most of the rest of the Senate thought otherwise. By majority vote, it decided to make war on Carthage, but it determined to await a pretext, and it kept its decision secret.

Rome's decision to fight, long before it was ready to fight, has some modern analogies. In 1911, Friedrich von Bernhardi, German general and military writer, expressed the view of Germany's war party that "France must be so completely crushed that she can never cross our path again." Even earlier, in 1909, the war party in Austria-Hungary had decided on war with Serbia, but had to convince both government and people, and find a pretext.

Adolf Hitler, according to Herman Rauschning, a German writer, confided to him in 1934 that he intended to fight England and France and added: "We must proceed step by step so that no one will impede our advance. . . . That it will be done is guaranteed by Britain's lack of firmness and France's disunity." And on November 5, 1937, Hitler informed the chiefs of his armed forces that Germany must make war on England and France before they were ready to fight.

Lenin pronounced the dictum that "the soundest strategy in war is to postpone operations until the moral disintegration of the enemy renders the delivery of the mortal blow both possible and easy."

Rome knew that long before Lenin.

And in the ensuing year, she behaved very much like Communist Russia during one of the thaws in the cold war.

The year after Cato's visit, a strange thing happened in Carthage. No Roman archives, no ancient historians explain the change in Roman policy. For the first time in nearly half a century, a Roman commission sent to Carthage to arbitrate her latest border dispute with Masinissa decided in favor of the astonished plaintiffs. Masinissa had to relinquish some of the property he had stolen.

Why did this happen? Certainly not because the anti-war Nasica headed the commission. The Senate always wrote the instructions for the delegations, so Nasica's decision undoubtedly represented national policy.

True, Rome still was in trouble in Spain, and in Liguria, in what is now the Alpes Maritimes of southern France and northwestern Italy. Rebellious tribes had crushingly defeated Roman armies, and, according to Livy, "had caused such confusion in the Roman state that no one could be found even to undertake service as military tribune or to accept a post as staff officer."

Certainly it was not a propitious time for another war. But

it was an excellent time for what we have come to call "psychological warfare," with its sudden shifts from "hard line" to "soft line" to gain immediate objectives and confound the opponent. Its name is new, but its techniques are not.

That year, Rome's interests required that Carthage remain quiet.

For one thing, Masinissa needed a year to prepare for his next mission against Carthage. Masinissa had led cavalry in the hit-and-run raids of guerrilla warfare and had served as chief of Numidian cavalry detachments in Roman armies. He had commanded no army of his own in a pitched battle, and never had laid siege to a city. He now had to be primed for an assignment of that magnitude. But no Cadmus would sow the seeds from which fully armed warriors would spring from the earth. Rome would have to supply arms and machines for siege operations and time would be needed for mobilization and training.

A second factor may have influenced Rome to shift her tactics. Although the Carthaginians had supinely bowed to Rome's "arbitration," their resentment at Roman support of Masinissa's thefts of territory had obviously been growing. Nasica's decision against Numidia would restore some of the prestige and power of the pro-Roman party in Carthage. Furthermore, it would lead the Carthaginians to believe that Rome would condone some resistance to additional Numidian depredations. Thus, eventually, and perhaps most importantly, it would provide Rome with the pretext she sought for a declaration of war.

Whether or not the Romans planned it that way, that is how it worked.

Nasica's decision and Masinissa's withdrawal from some Carthaginian territory altered the balance of power among Carthage's political parties. The pro-Roman party gained and the pro-Masinissa faction lost strength. But it was the democratic "Carthage-firsters" of the national people's party who were able to force action. They considered Masinissa the greatest and most immediate danger to Carthage and they compelled the Popular Assembly to vote to exile the forty leaders of the pro-Masinissa party, and to pledge that it would never take them back, or even discuss taking them back.

The exiles sought refuge with Masinissa, and urged him to declare war on their native land.

Appian compresses the history of those momentous events of the winter and the spring of 151-150 B.C. in these few sentences:

[Masinissa], nothing loath, sent two of his sons, Gulussa and Micipsa, to Carthage to demand that those who had been expelled on his account should be taken back. When they came to the city gates, the commanding officer of the mercenary forces shut them out, fearing lest the relatives of the exiles should prevail with the multitude by their tears. As Gulussa was returning, Hamilcar the Samnite set upon him, killed some of his attendants, and thoroughly frightened him. Thereupon Masinissa, making this an excuse, laid siege to the town of Oroscopa, which he desired to possess contrary to the treaty. The Carthaginians with 25,000 foot and 400 city horse under Hasdrubal, who then commanded the mercenaries, marched against Masinissa. At their approach, Asasis and Suba, Masinissa's lieutenants, on account of some differences with his sons, deserted with 6,000 horse. Encouraged by this accession, Hasdrubal moved his forces nearer to the king and in some skirmishes gained the advantage. But Masinissa, laying a trap for him, retired little by little as if in flight, until he had drawn him into a great desert surrounded by hills and crags, and destitute of provisions. Then turning about he pitched his camp in the open plain, but Hasdrubal drew up among the hills as being a stronger position.

Masinissa's feigned retreat from his siege of Oroscopa showed brilliant strategic skill. Evidently he had not missed the point of Scipio's maneuver before the battle of Zama fifty-two years earlier. Then, Scipio the Elder, by his inland maneuver, had prevented Hannibal from offering battle in the vicinity of Carthage.

Hannibal had had sound reason to follow him and to seek battle before Scipio and Masinissa joined forces. But Scipio's strategy had deprived Hannibal of the strong pivot of maneuver which the city of Carthage constituted, and had cut him off from access to its well-stocked base—an impregnable refuge if his comparatively weak army met defeat in battle.

Masinissa counted on gaining a similar advantage by his withdrawal in this campaign. It was an old stratagem, older than Scipio the Elder. When Masinissa retreated, Hasdrubal, obviously elated at having acquired the Numidian cavalry deserters and at having won some skirmishes, unhesitatingly pursued. Thus far, in following Masinissa and attempting to bring him to battle, he was right. But Masinissa, as though in fear of the Carthaginian army, continued to withdraw. His purpose was to lure Hasdrubal farther and farther away from his base and, presumably, closer to Masinissa's own.

Hasdrubal followed too far, violating the first principle of generalship so clearly defined by Socrates, who was a soldier as well as a philosopher: "A general must be capable of getting military equipment and providing supplies for his men." The two armies paused in a desert surrounded by hills and crags and destitute of provisions. Masinissa camped in the plain. But Carthaginian armies had an irresistible and inordinate desire for security and pitched their camps on high hills, which are easier to defend. This preoccupation with a strong defensive position had brought them almost irremediable disaster in the First Punic War: cavalry and elephants fight better on level ground. Nevertheless, Hasdrubal camped in the hills.

The battle fought the day after the two armies encamped has been little noted in history, but in its circumstances and consequences it ranks among the most extraordinary. One of its curious aspects was that a host marched into combat led by an eighty-eight-year-old king who had never before enjoyed full command in a major conflict. Another was that a young man present as a noncombatant spectator lived to confront and defeat one of the contending generals, and destroy the capital city which he served.

The witness was Scipio Africanus the Younger, grandson of the Scipio Africanus beside whom Masinissa had fought Hannibal at Zama. He had come from the Roman army headquarters in Spain to procure elephants from Masinissa for use against the rebellious tribes. He had reached the battlefield too late to meet Masinissa, who had begun moving into the field. But Masinissa had detailed some of his many sons and a cavalry escort to receive him and to take him to a vantage point on one of the surrounding hills. Scipio Africanus the Younger thus enjoyed a marvelous view of the gladiatorial contest of 110,000 men in the amphitheater below, and in his later years he used to say that only Jupiter from Mount Ida and Neptune from Samothrace had also witnessed such a scene. This is what he saw:

Beginning at dawn, Masinissa on horseback personally led each large unit of his 55,000-man army from camp to its position on the line. Then Hasdrubal moved his 58,000 men down from their hilltop camp and drew them up in battle array facing the Numidians. Though Hasdrubal's force slightly outnumbered Masinissa's, Hasdrubal's cavalry totaled only 6,400, of whom 6,000 were Numidian deserters and the remainder Carthaginian members of the capital's troop of nobles in shining armor. Masinissa unquestionably counted more horsemen, and the terrain ideally suited cavalry conflict: that was why Masinissa had chosen the plain for a battleground.

The two lines soon clashed. The combat lasted from a little after dawn to nightfall. Though Hasdrubal's cavalry was outnumbered, the Numidian deserters must have fought with an extra ferocity born of hatred, for Appian reports merely that "it seemed that Masinissa had the advantage," words he would not have used to describe a decisive victory.

The aftermath of the battle proved as strange as its other aspects. Masinissa warmly welcomed Scipio Africanus the Younger and when the Carthaginians learned of the Roman's presence, Appian reports, "they besought Scipio to make terms for them with Masinissa." Though they had hardly been defeated, they offered to surrender their claims to the territory around Emporium, already seized by Masinissa, and to pay a heavy war indemnity. But with surprising courage they rejected Masinissa's demand that they surrender the survivors of the 6,000 Numidian cavalrymen who had fought on Carthage's side. So the conference failed and Scipio returned to Spain with the elephants for which he had come.

Masinissa then proceeded with a plan to destroy the enemy he had not quite beaten in battle. He set his men to digging trenches around the foot of the hill occupied by Hasdrubal's camp, cutting it off from supplies and making it difficult for Hasdrubal's force to move. Still healthy and strong, Hasdrubal's army could have broken through the line had Hasdrubal given the word. But Hasdrubal did not. He estimated that he had more supplies on hand than did Masinissa, and calculated that he could outsit him. Furthermore, he had heard that a peace delegation was on its way from Rome, and since the 152 B.C. delegation which Nasica had headed had not been unfavorable to Carthage, he had good reason to hope. He would not have been so sanguine if he had known the instructions that the delegation of 150 B.C. had been given. According to Appian their orders were: "If Masinissa were beaten, to put an end to the strife, but if he were successful to spur him on."

So the siege continued. Food gave out in Hasdrubal's camp, and water was scarce in those arid hills. Hasdrubal's men slaughtered their pack animals and their horses for meat; when that source vanished, they boiled their leather straps to eat. They began to die of hunger, thirst, and disease. Soon they lacked even wood for burning corpses, and space in which to bury them.

Despairing of escape or rescue by a force from Carthage, Hasdrubal finally agreed to surrender the Numidian deserters, to pay a heavy war indemnity, and to take back the friends of Masinissa who had been exiled from Carthage—something the Carthaginians had sworn never to do.

By the terms of the surrender, the staggering survivors were to leave their camp one by one through a single gate, taking with them only a tunic apiece, and to walk—as best they could— through a long corridor formed by their enemies. What happened next may have been the idea not of Masinissa but of his son Gulussa, still wrathful at the assault he had suffered the year before upon leaving Carthage. As the sick and starved survivors of Hasdrubal's army dragged themselves out of their camp, Numidian cavalry massacred them. "So out of 58,000 men composing the army," Appian reports, "only a few returned to Carthage, among them Hasdrubal, the general, and others of the nobility."

IX

THE COLD WAR ENDS:

150-149 B.C.

Without too much difficulty Carthage could assuage its grief at the loss of some 50,000 more or less expendable mercenaries. But most of the gallant four hundred young men detached from the aristocratic Sacred Band also had perished. Militarily, the destruction of Hasdrubal's army left Carthage at least temporarily helpless. Psychologically, it drained the national morale of will to resist. Diplomatically, it left her without a chance of finding allies. None would be so foolish as to sign an alliance with a moribund land. For Rome, the outcome had been a triumph of cold-war strategy. Without committing a single Roman soldier, she had won, through a satellite, a tremendous victory.

Nevertheless cold-war diplomacy had become too slow; it demanded patience. In the years immediately before and after 150, Rome's foreign policy changed from the slow procedure she had used for decades against Carthage to a more militant and aggressive imperialism. Her large landholders on their slave-operated *latifundia* (estates) made available for extended military service many more peasants who shared in the loot of conquest. The senatorial class was eager for military distinction. The commercial and financial community had grown in size and political power and profited from the new Roman provinces in the fruits of victory.

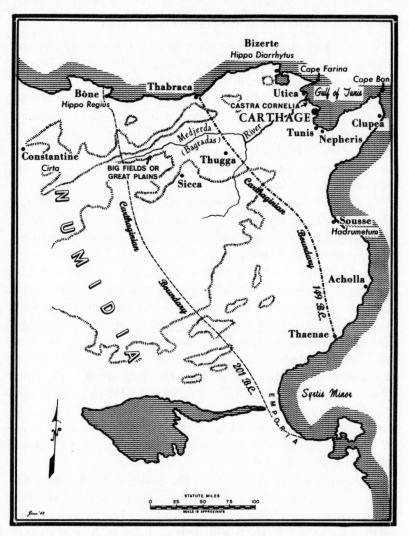

Carthaginian boundaries after the Second (201 B.C.) and at the start
of the Third (149 B.C.) Punic Wars. The Carthaginians were gradually wedged into a narrow strip of land along the sea as the Numidian
king, with Rome's support, used cold war tactics to seize, slice by
slice, the territory between the two boundaries. (Based on data from
Stéphane Gsell's *Histoire Ancienne de l'Afrique du Nord*.)

Rome's goal of a dominant position in the Mediterranean was evident to her prospective victims. Macedonia in northern Greece, the Greek city-states south of the Gulf of Corinth, the strong island republic of Rhodes, and Syria and Egypt all had reason to be apprehensive of Roman imperialism. These were Carthage's potential allies in the Mediterranean world; but when or where is it possible to find in the annals of the past any concerted effort by prospective victims to stop an aggressor until it was too late or nearly too late?

In its mourning for its young nobles and for its own plight, Carthage assigned the culpability to Hasdrubal, and an earlier, tougher generation would have crucified him without delay. Certainly much of the blame was his. He had led his army into a trap. He had fought and scarcely failed in battle, but had feared to fight a second day and had offered to pay a tremendous price for not fighting. If he judged that he could not win a return engagement, he could have done as General Lee did after Antietam. Facing McClellan's superior strength, Lee abandoned the invasion of Maryland, withdrew into Virginia, shortened his line of communications, and awaited a more favorable opportunity to fight. Hasdrubal chose to sit besieged on his hilltop. He showed courage, it is true, in refusing to turn over the Numidian cavalry deserters to Masinissa. But he lacked the courage to try to break the siege. A Roman military tribune named Decius, in a similar situation, behaved quite differently.

In Rome's war of conquest on the Samnite people of central Italy which took fifty-three years to win, Decius, for strategic reasons, occupied a hilltop with a small force. Decius and his men found themselves besieged and without hope of help from outside. So, Livy reports, Decius addressed his men:

It cannot be a question now, whether you ought to stay here or march away from this place, seeing that fortune has left you nothing but your arms and courage to use them. We must die by hunger and thirst, if we dread the sword of the enemy more than becomes brave men and Romans. The only way to save ourselves is to cut our way through them and march off.

And this they did, breaking out at night through a far larger force surrounding the hill.

Hasdrubal was no Decius. He chose for his men death by hunger and thirst, and in the end, he negated, by turning over the Numidian deserters, the one courageous thing he had done.

Certainly, Masinissa proved himself the better general. But in mitigation of Hasdrubal's behavior, it should be said that he may have acted as he did out of a timidity inspired by Carthaginian military policy, which made Carthaginian generals fear their own countrymen almost as much as they feared the enemy. When one knew that the penalty of defeat was crucifixion by the people one defended, one avoided the risk of defeat by avoiding combat whenever possible. Hasdrubal's name, incidentally, means "he who has the help of Baal." But Baal, like rival gods, helps those who help themselves, and there was nothing in Hasdrubal's conduct to encourage divine intercession.

Nevertheless, Carthage did not crucify Hasdrubal. The new, supine generation which ruled the city had a better idea: why not deliver Hasdrubal's corpse as a sacrificial offering to Rome? Carthaginian intelligence agents had reported a general mobilization in Italy. If the blame for the war on Masinissa could be shifted to a few scapegoats, Hasdrubal among them, Carthage might be spared further ignominy. So just as they had attempted to cast the entire blame for the Second Punic War on Hannibal, the Carthaginians now "condemned Hasdrubal . . . and any others who were concerned in the matter, to death, putting the whole blame of the war upon them."

But Hasdrubal, showing as always a prodigious instinct for survival, escaped with the other officers sentenced to death. Hasdrubal's escape added to Carthage's worries. In 150 B.C. enemies menaced the city from every direction. Masinissa had his army in the field, and stood as an immediate threat. Rome and her Italian allies were mobilizing troops "for emergencies." And Carthage feared that Hasdrubal would gather an army to inflict revenge on the helpless nation which had condemned him.

Something had to be done. Carthage's first move was to send an embassy to Rome to complain about Masinissa's invasion of her territory and, with an abjectness that must have disgusted the Romans, to charge Hasdrubal and other Carthaginian officers with "taking up arms against him too hastily and rashly, and of furnishing an occasion for an imputation of hostility on the part of their city," as Appian records it. "When one of the senators inquired: 'Why didn't you condemn these officers at the beginning of the war instead of waiting till they were beaten? Why didn't you send this embassy earlier, instead of postponing it?' the embassy was silent.

"The Senate *which had previously resolved upon war* [italics supplied], and was only seeking some petty excuse, answered that the defense so far offered by the Carthaginians was not satisfactory. The latter, much disturbed, asked again, if they had done wrong, how would they atone for it. The answer was brief: 'You must satisfy the Roman people.'"

The exchange took place probably about September 150 B.C. It began a period of negotiations in which Rome played cat to Carthage's mouse. In the first and in succeeding "conferences" Rome talked always in enigmas and ambiguities. For fifty years, Carthage had been marching toward doom at half-step. But Masinissa's victory had whetted Rome's imperialistic appetite. Rome now quickened the pace. And Carthage, innocent of the price of appeasement, tried to buy salvation by offering more and more.

The Carthaginian delegation returned home from the first mission perplexed by the Roman reply. The Carthaginian Senate debated its meaning. What could satisfy the Roman people? Carthage had paid the fiftieth and final installment of the reparations agreed to in the peace treaty of 201. Would Rome be satisfied by a new indemnity? Or by the surrender of the disputed territory to Masinissa?

A second embassy went to Rome to request specific peace conditions. Satisfaction for Rome? The Romans replied that "the Carthaginians knew perfectly well" what that meant and sent them home, still bewildered.

Rome had won a military victory by using a satellite. She had confused and baffled her enemy by psychological warfare after that victory. Now she turned to a third cold-war device, subversion.

Utica, second in size and importance only to Carthage and a mere twenty miles from the capital, would prove immensely useful to Rome as a base in any action against Carthage: the strongly fortified city had port and ship-repair facilities, and a plenitude of skilled labor. And her loyalty to Carthage was questionable. In the War of the Mercenaries, Utica had offered to surrender to Rome, and though Rome rejected the proposal for reasons of policy, Utica had joined the mutineers. In the Second Punic War, however, Utica had remained loyal to Carthage and had beaten off all Roman efforts to take the city by storm or by blockade.

In February of 149 B.C., Utica abruptly defected from Carthage and made her ports and their facilities available to Rome. The news shocked Carthage, but failed to surprise Rome, which had had agents busy in the city. What alluring prize they had dangled before the Uticans remains unrecorded: perhaps they promised that Utica would replace Carthage as head of state. But obviously the price was high enough.

Correctly interpreting Utica's treachery as an omen of a Roman threat of war, the desperate Carthaginians convened the Senate in secret session. What to do? Polybius writes that the Carthaginians could only choose between "two evils, either to accept war with brave hearts or to entrust themselves to the faith of Rome," a Roman euphemism for unconditional surrender.

"Not even in the season of their greatest danger," Polybius continues, "when they had been utterly defeated, and the enemy was at their gates had they ever thus surrendered the liberty of their country."

Having discussed alternatives, the Carthaginian Senate appointed plenipotentiaries to go to Rome with authority "to do whatever they thought was in the interest of their country under present circumstances." In other words, surrender unconditionally, if necessary.

While Carthage talked, Rome acted. Carthage's envoys reached Rome only to learn that the Roman Senate, meeting in the Capitol, in March 149 had declared war. It had been a close thing, though. Nasica's anti-war party apparently had developed considerable strength and influence, and Polybius, recalling that the Romans long ago had decided on war but had been determined first to find "a pretext that would appeal to foreign nations," records that "on this occasion their dispute with each other about the effect on foreign opinion very nearly made them desist from going to war."

Despite the reservations of Nasica and his supporters, war had been voted, and Rome's generals, with their armies, were on their way to Utica and Carthage. The Carthaginian envoys faced a *fait accompli*, and "as the situation left them no choice," they committed Carthage to the faith of Rome, i.e., they surrendered unconditionally.

It seemed, in fact, a good deal, on the basis of Roman promises. Polybius writes:

Shortly after this surrender had been made by the Carthaginians, they were called into the Senate, where the praetor conveyed to them the decision of the Senate, that as they had been well advised, THE SENATE GRANTED THEM FREEDOM AND THEIR LAWS, BESIDES THEIR WHOLE TERRITORY AND ALL OTHER POSSESSIONS BOTH PUBLIC AND PRIVATE [emphasis mine, D.A.]. *The Carthaginians on hearing this* were pleased, thinking that in the choice of evils they had been well treated by the Senate, as all that was most essential and important had been conceded to them.

The praetor informed them that these were the peace terms provided that within thirty days they delivered to the Roman consuls three hundred hostages, sons of the senators and other distinguished Carthaginians, and "if they obeyed the orders of the consuls."

The envoys agreed, confident that they had nothing to fear, not even any orders of the consuls.

The envoys' trust was tragically misplaced. Driven by what Polybius described as "lust of domination," Rome's chicanery offended at least some neutral opinion, which charged that "throughout the whole of their proceedings in regard to Carthage, they [the Romans] had used deceit and fraud, offering certain things one at a time and keeping others secret until they cut off every hope the city had of help from her allies. This, they said, savored more of a despot's intrigue than of the principles of a civilized state such as Rome, and could only be justly described as something very like impiety and treachery."

And treachery it was. Little time had been lost between the declaration of war and the Senate's order for the two consuls of that year to embark the Roman Expeditionary Force, which consisted of 80,000 infantry and 4,000 cavalry commanded by Marcus Manilius, and a fleet of fifty quinquiremes and the necessary transports under L. Marcius Censorinus. What was their mission? Before the consuls embarked, the Senate "gave them secret orders," Appian writes, "not to desist from the war until Carthage was razed to the ground." [Italics supplied.] After the Carthaginian envoys accepted the peace terms, the Senate sent "word privately to the consuls that they should carry out their secret instructions."

Impatiently, Carthage awaited the return of the third peace

mission, and at last the galley sailed into the harbor and the envoys came ashore. This time there was no puzzling ultimatum that only heightened worry and demoralization. The envoys had agreed to unconditional surrender. But Rome had promised Carthage freedom and the retention of her territory and of her public and private property. Perhaps the pro-Roman party had been right after all.

Then came the cruel blow for the Carthaginian aristocracy—the demand for three hundred hostages. Already, for nearly a year, Carthage's leading families had been mourning the dead in the Sacred Band of Hasdrubal's army. Now nearly every noble family would lose at least one more son. And as usual, Roman demands contained that one additional cruel twist: nothing had been said about the hostages' return.

Although this meant for most of them the personal 'loss of a son, Carthage's senators decreed immediate selection and departure of the hostages; swift compliance might soften Roman hearts. Polybius writes that without delay they chose "three hundred of their young men [and] dispatched them with great lamentations and tears, as each was escorted by his near friends and relatives, the women being especially violent in their grief."

Appian elaborates, perhaps inventively:

So, hastily anticipating the appointed time, they sent their children into Sicily, amid the tears of the parents, the kindred, and especially the mothers, who clung to their little ones with frantic cries and seized hold of the ships and of the officers who were taking them away, even holding the anchors and tearing the ropes, and throwing their arms around the sailors in order to prevent the ships from moving; some of them even swam far out into the sea beside the ships, shedding tears and gazing at their children. Others on the shore tore out their hair and smote their breasts as though they were mourning the dead. For it seemed to them that the giving of hostages was a mere specious phrase,

which meant really the giving up of the city, when they surrendered their children without any fixed conditions. Many of
them predicted, with lamentations, that it would profit the city
nothing to have delivered up their children. Such were the scenes
that took place in Carthage when the hostages were sent away.
When the consuls received them in Sicily they sent them to
Rome, and said to the Carthaginians that IN REFERENCE TO THE
ENDING OF THE WAR THEY WOULD GIVE THEM FURTHER INFORMATION
AT UTICA. [Emphasis mine, D.A.]

The intuition of the Carthaginian mothers was correct: never
again would they see their sons.

Carthage knew that "further information" meant more demands.
The Carthaginians had counted on each step in their appeasement
of Rome to end their torment. Each time they had appeased in
vain. And the worst was yet to come. It began with blackmail by
terror.

The Roman expeditionary force had pitched camp two miles
west of Utica, on a long, narrow, fairly high, steep-sided promontory extending into the Gulf of Tunis, and field fortifications
made it virtually impregnable to direct attack or siege. It was
called Castra Cornelia, after Publius Cornelius Scipio Africanus,
who had camped there in the Second Punic War.

To Castra Cornelia went Carthage's envoys, headed by a
spokesman named Banno. The Roman consuls had prepared for
them with a spectacular exhibition of Roman military might.
Lining the long road from the camp gate to the dais where the
consuls waited, the 80,000 Roman infantrymen and the 4,000
horsemen stood at attention. Each legion displayed its silver
eagle, each cohort a standard mounting a bronze animal, each
cavalry unit its banner. Swords and spears, helmets and shields
gleamed in the spring sun. Trumpets sounded fanfares as the
envoys slowly advanced.

Surrounded by tribunes and other aides, the counsuls sat behind ropes arranged to keep the suppliants at their distance, and haughtily ordered the Carthaginians to state their requests.

Banno pleaded for reconciliation and clemency. Rome, he argued, had not needed to declare war or to send its army and fleet, for the Carthaginians had already surrendered. For fifty years they had faithfully fulfilled the terms of the old peace treaty, and now they were ready to submit to any penalty; this they had proved by giving the hostages. He enumerated Carthage's acts of appeasement. True, the Carthaginians had taken up arms against Masinissa, but that had been a natural reaction to the seizure of their territory. And had they not condemned to death the officers who had caused the war? Now they prayed for mercy and moderation, and reminded the consuls of Rome's promise that "Carthage should remain free under her own laws and in the enjoyment of her possessions."

In the Roman tradition, the Consul Censorinus responded ambiguously, then came to the point—or the first of his points. "If you sincerely desire peace," he said, "why do you need any arms? Come, surrender to us all your weapons and war equipment, both public and private."

The Carthaginians apparently promised to comply, but meekly pointed out that they would be defenseless against Hasdrubal, who had gathered an army of 20,000 men and threatened Carthage. Leave that to us, the consuls answered.

The consuls named two senators to supervise Carthage's disarmament; one was Nasica, and perhaps his presence inspired the Carthaginians to hope they would be treated justly. The Carthaginians collected and turned over to the Roman commission two hundred thousand complete sets of soldiers' equipment—helmets, shields, breastplates, greaves (shin guards), and weapons—swords and spears. In addition, they gave up two thousand catapults, which could hurl stone projectiles or heavy arrows as far as five hundred yards, and "innumerable javelins and darts." The Romans were incredulous, and Appian comments that "it was a remarkable and unparalleled spectacle to behold the vast number of loaded wagons which the enemy themselves brought in."

When the Roman armistice commission returned to Utica to report that all the arms had been delivered, the consuls summoned the Carthaginian delegation to hear the final condition for a peace treaty. This time Carthage had augmented its negotiators with "leading senators and citizens, priests and other distinguished persons, who hoped to inspire the consuls with respect or pity for them." They stood before the consuls with bowed heads.

Censorinus rose. Frowning, he gazed long and silently at the Carthaginians. Then he said:

Your ready obedience up to this point, Carthaginians, in the matter of the hostages and the arms, is worthy of all praise. But in cases of necessity, we must not multiply words. Bear bravely the remaining command of the Senate. Yield Carthage to us, and betake yourselves where you like within your own territory at a distance of at least ten miles from the sea, for we are resolved to raze your city to the ground.

The cringing suppliants straightened in fury. Tension against Rome had been mounting during the weeks of surrender, first of their children, then of their arms. Helpless, and few among thousands of armed men, the Carthaginians "virulently cursed the Romans, either because they wished to die, or because they were out of their minds, or because they were determined to provoke the Romans to sacrilegious violence to ambassadors. They flung themselves on the ground. . . . When at last the frenzy was past they lay there, crushed and silent like dead men." Even the Romans were moved.

It had taken the Carthaginians only seconds to realize the significance of Censorinus's words. Obedience meant the loss of their homes and occupations, their commercial and naval harbors, their maritime commerce and their industries, their temples and their public buildings. To build another Carthage would be a task of years, and without their city walls, how could they defend themselves against Masinissa and Utica?

An even more powerful motive may have animated them. Their gods dwelt in their temples, and beyond their material pursuits the Carthaginians, like their Phoenician ancestors, had only one interest: religion. They played no games, and they eschewed theaters and circuses. They looked to their gods to protect their cities and their commerce, their cattle and their crops, their health and their homes, and they profoundly revered their shrines.

Materialism had motivated Carthage's repeated appeasement of Rome. Now appeasement was to cost the Carthaginians the homes of their gods. The price was too high. Whatever moderns may think of the Carthaginian religion, it was to the Carthaginians a spiritual force which was to arouse in them the fervor of a crusade.

Before dismissing the envoys, the consuls agreed to hear Banno. He said:

If you still have any respect for what we have said to you before, Romans, we will speak, not as though we were contending for right (since disputation is never timely for the unfortunate), but that you may perceive that pity on your part toward us is not without excuse and not without reason. We were once the rulers of Africa and of the greater part of the sea, and contended with yourselves for empire. We desisted from this in the time of Scipio, when we gave up to you all the ships and elephants we had. We agreed to pay you tribute and we pay it at the appointed time. Now, in the name of the gods who witnessed the oaths, spare us, respect the oath sworn by Scipio that the Romans and Carthaginians should be allies and friends. We have not violated the treaty. We have no ships, no elephants. The tribute is not in default. On the contrary, we have fought on your side against three kings. . . . [Banno's reference was to the assistance Carthage gave Rome when the Romans were fighting King Philip V of

Macedon (200-196), King Antiochus of Syria (192-189) and King Perseus of Macedon (171-167). Livy records that the Carthaginians sent naval forces, as well as huge shipments of grain, which in 170 B.C. alone amounted to one million pecks of wheat and 500,000 of barley. Carthage made a whole-hearted effort, rare on the part of the vanquished, to build a better peace.]

You asked hostages, and we gave you our best. You asked for our arms, and you have received them all, which even captured cities do not willingly give up. We had confidence in the Romans' habits and character. Your Senate sent us word, and you confirmed it, when the hostages were demanded, that if they were delivered, Carthage should be left free and autonomous. If it was added that we should endure your further commands it was not to be expected that in the matter of the hostages you would, in your distinct demand, promise that the city should be independent, and then besides the hostages would make a further demand that Carthage itself be destroyed. If it is right for you to destroy it, how can you leave it free and autonomous as you said you would? . . .

We beseech you, in behalf of an ancient city founded by command of the gods, in behalf of a glory that has become great and a name that has pervaded the whole world, in behalf of the many temples it contains and of its gods who have done you no wrong. Do not deprive them of their nightly festivals, their processions and their solemnities. Deprive not the tombs of the dead, who harm you no more, of their offerings. If you have pity for us (as you say that out of pity you yield us another dwelling-place), spare the city's hearth, spare our forum, spare the goddess who presides over our council, and all else that is dear and precious to the living. What fear can you have of Carthage when you are in possession of our ships and our arms and the elephants which you grudge us? As to a change of dwelling-place (if that is considered in the light of a consolation), it is impracticable for our people, a countless number of whom get their living by the sea, to move into the country. We propose an alternative more desirable for us and more glorious for you. Spare the city which has done you no harm, but, if you please, kill us, whom you have ordered to move away. In this way you will seem to vent your wrath upon men, not upon temples, gods, tombs, and an innocent city.

Romans, you desire a good name and reputation for piety in all that you do, and you profess the virtue of moderation in prosperity, and claim credit for it from those whom you conquer. Do not, I implore you in the name of Jove and of the other gods, especially those who still preside over Carthage (and may they never bear a grudge against you or your children), do not tarnish your own good name for the first time in your dealings with us. Do not defile your reputation by an act so horrible to do and to hear, and which you will be the first in history to perform. Greeks and barbarians have waged many wars, and you, Romans, have waged many against other nations, but no one has ever razed to the ground a city whose people had surrendered before the fight and delivered up their arms and children, and submitted to every other penalty that could be imposed upon men. Reminding you of the oaths sworn before the gods, of the mutability of the human lot, and Nemesis, most terrible to the fortunate, we beseech you not to do violence to your own fair record, and not to increase our calamities beyond all cure.

Banno concluded his eloquent plea with a request for permission to send another embassy to Rome. Perhaps the Senate might receive favorably their petition to preserve the city.

Censorinus rose to reply. Stern and unyielding, he began by reminding the Carthaginians that he was acting under orders of the Roman Senate. Discussion was useless. He argued merely to convince the delegation that Carthage's destruction would benefit the Carthaginians. He said:

The sea reminds you of the dominion and power you once acquired by means of it. It prompts you to wrongdoing and brings you thus into disaster. The sea made you invade Sicily and lose it again. Then you invaded Spain and were driven out of it. . . . You lost Sardinia also because of the sea, which always begets a grasping disposition by the very facilities which it offers for gain. . . . Believe me, Carthaginians, life inland, with the joys of agriculture and quiet, is much more equable. Although the gains of agriculture are, perhaps, smaller than those of mercantile life, they are surer and a great deal safer.

The Carthaginians ought to be grateful to the Romans, he went on, for removing them from temptation. He pointed out that the new Carthage could be built only ten miles from the sea, and reminded them that Rome was twelve miles from the coast.

In speciousness, Censorinus was matchless—until, perhaps, Hitler and the Russian and Chinese Communists. He concluded with a morsel of Roman generosity:

We offer you whatever place you choose to take, and when you have taken it you shall live under your own laws. This is what we told you beforehand, that Carthage should have her own laws if you would obey our commands. We considered you to be Carthage, not the ground where you live.

Censorinus paused, and the Carthaginians remained in stunned silence. Then he dismissed the delegation with these words:

All that can be said in the way of persuasion and consolation has been said. The order of the Senate must be carried out, and quickly, too. Therefore, take your departure, for you are still ambassadors.

But the delegates feared to go home with such evil tidings. To prevent violence to themselves at their countrymen's hands, they asked the Romans to send a fleet to Carthage. Humiliated and ashamed, they ended: "To this state has fortune and necessity brought us that we ourselves ask you to hasten your ships against our fatherland."

The Romans granted the favor: a task force of their fleet anchored near the city.

But the envoys had predicted correctly the wild and wrathful disorder that the Roman ultimatum occasioned. It was the Pearl Harbor that united a passive and unresisting people and transformed it into a resolute and courageous, if helpless, nation.

X

CARTHAGE GOES TO WAR

The sun was about to disappear behind the western mountains. A growing crowd massed atop Carthage's walls and towers to peer toward Utica. There was room enough on the ramparts for hundreds to stand where batteries of the now surrendered catapults had defended the city a few days earlier. The crowd on the walls saw many of their fellow citizens, even more impatient to hear the news, walking or riding out on the Utica road to meet the peace mission.

A shout went up. On the high hill which hid Utica from Carthage, a cloud of dust arose from the road. The delegates were in sight. But they still had a long way to go, and, heartbroken and frightened, they were in no hurry. They refused to answer questions put by the first citizens to meet them, but their downcast eyes and tragic faces, and the fact that a number of the envoys were not in the returning delegation bespoke the worst. But no one yet guessed what that worst was.

Finally the envoys stood before the Senate assembled in executive session. They announced the edict of destruction. So loud was the senators' wrathful outcry that the people outside heard it. Again there was silence. The delegation was reporting its request to send an embassy to Rome and the consuls' refusal. Again, the sound of lamentation from the Senate chamber reached the people's ears. The agony of uncertainty was too much for the crowd.

93

They overwhelmed the guards and rushed to the Senate floor. They heard the dreadful news. Appian, with some usual rhetorical exaggeration, describes their frenzy:

Then followed a scene of blind, raving madness, like the strange acts which the Maenads are said to perform when under the influence of Bacchus. Some fell upon those senators who had advised giving the hostages and tore them in pieces, considering them the ones who had led them into the trap. Others treated in a similar way those who had favored giving up the arms. Some stoned the ambassadors for bringing the bad news, and others dragged them through the city. Still others, meeting certain Italians who were caught among them in this sudden and unexpected mischance, maltreated them in various ways, adding that they would make them suffer for the fraud practiced upon them in the matter of the hostages and the arms. The city was full of wailing and wrath, of fear and threatenings. People roamed the streets invoking whatever was most dear to them and took refuge in the temples as in asylums. They upbraided their gods for not even being able to defend themselves. Some went into the arsenals and wept when they found them empty. Others ran to the dockyards and bewailed the ships that had been surrendered [after the Second Punic War] to perfidious men. Some called their elephants by name, as though they were still there, and reviled their own ancestors and themselves for not perishing, sword in hand, with their country, without paying tribute and giving up their elephants, their ships, and their arms. Most of all was their anger kindled by the mothers of the hostages who, like Furies in a tragedy, accosted those whom they met with shrieks, and reproached them with giving away their children against their protest, or mocked at them, saying that the gods were now taking vengeance on them for the lost children. The few who remained sane closed the gates, and brought stones upon the walls to be used in place of catapults.

In the spring of 149 B.C. Rome had reduced Carthage to total impotence. But that was not enough. Rome, as Diodorus Siculus explains, had resolved that her purpose of world domination would be advanced by a policy of "paralyzing terror to secure it against attack." Carthage would be wiped out to prove to the world the futility of resisting Roman aggression. This time, however, Rome had gone too far.

The fury of the citizens is understandable. To deprive Carthage of access to the Mediterranean meant economic death to the nation and physical death to most of the city's inhabitants. How could a population of that size be removed to a new site without long preparation? There were no water supplies, no shelter, no building materials, no roads and no streets, no vehicles for transporting such a population. The Roman argument that Carthage could build a new city only ten miles from the sea while Rome itself was twelve miles inland was cynical sophistry. Rome was on the Tiber, a river navigable up to the city. The Medjerda, the largest river in Carthaginian territory, was too shallow for navigation.

But the Roman ultimatum meant the end of the Carthaginian economy. Years would be needed to build a new seaport like Rome's Ostia and Athens's Piraeus with harbors, docks, warehouses, shipbuilding ways, and houses and utilities for the people. Moreover, Carthage grew rich from a tax on all merchandise entering and leaving port. She depended on transit trade—silver, tin, and other metals from the west to markets in Egypt and farther east. The choice for Carthage was death in combat or death by slow attrition.

The populace clamored for war, and that night the Senate declared war. The Senators renounced their luxury. They passed a law to free the slaves. They elected generals. The Senate sent messengers to Hasdrubal, who had mobilized a personal army of thirty thousand men outside the city walls, begged him to forget the sentence of death which they had imposed on him in their efforts to appease Rome, and urged him to head a defensive force to prevent the Roman army from destroying the rich agricultural resources of the Cape Bon peninsula, whose grain and meat could keep Carthage alive. Hasdrubal consented. He fortified a camp for his army near the strong hill town of Nepheris controlling the road to Cape Bon.

On that day of decision nobody in Rome or in Carthage could have anticipated the outcome unless he remembered the history and the national character of Tyre and Carthage.

The past is the prologue to explain the imminent turning point in the tragedy of the life and death of Carthage. In preceding chapters Rome and Carthage have disclosed their characters, their psychological traits, their moral strength and weakness, their natural advantages and disadvantages, the conflict of wills in the four Punic Wars and in the cold war. That history has proved that neither Tyre nor Carthage ever really put their hearts and their total resources into the defense of their honor and dignity, their freedom and their very existence, until a powerful and ruthless enemy stood at the very gates of the city.

In Rome, militarism had captured decision-making and had caused this cruel and senseless decree of Carthage's execution. In Carthage, peace-at-any-price appeasement had made Rome's task easy. It had led to unconditional surrender and total, unilateral disarmament. Surely Carthage could expect that now the Roman legions would return to Italy and once more Carthage could turn her attention to gathering the rich fruits of foreign commerce.

The Senate made another shrewd decision. It chose as commanding general in the city the son of a Carthaginian-Numidian marriage: the new general's mother was a daughter of Masinissa. Undoubtedly this selection was politically motivated. Appian reports that "Masinissa was vexed with the Romans, and took it hard to hear that when he had brought the Carthaginians to their knees others should carry off the glory before his eyes, not even communicating with him beforehand, as they had done in other wars." Might not the appointment of Masinissa's grandson to supreme command in the city of Carthage persuade the old king —now almost ninety—to join forces with his ancient enemy?

The newly appointed general, too, was named Hasdrubal. The Carthaginians apparently had few names to choose from and were usually content with a single name. To prevent confusion between the two Hasdrubals, we shall call the general in Carthage, Hasdrubal Numidianus, with the warning that this surname will be found in no other book.

The siege of Carthage was about to begin. For the Carthaginians it was a crusade for survival, for the right and the ability to live, for the defense of their gods, their temples, and their homes. The old leaders of appeasement were deposed. Some were killed. No military clique in Carthage had urged war. The decision to resist was the people's. *No war before or since failed so absolutely to be a continuation of national policy. Policy had been appeasement. War had been abandoned as an instrument of policy. This was a spontaneous and sudden shift from unconditional surrender to dogged and enduring defiance.*

No nation has ever declared war against greater odds. With not a man in her defenses or a weapon in her arsenals, with not a ship in her navy, with scarcely a friend and with no allies, Carthage prepared to take on the world's strongest power. Eighty-four thousand Romans under arms stood nearby, with a fleet offshore and Masinissa was not far away.

The situation, however, was not hopeless. Carthage knew that tension between Masinissa and the Roman consuls was increasing. Hasdrubal's patriotism having proved stronger than his anger, Carthage could count on him for an exterior threat to the Roman army. Moreover, Rome was already fighting hard in Spain and had many enemies, as we have seen. There was hope for a coalition against her. A siege, furthermore, was the most costly, the most demoralizing of all military operations. Prolonged, it would lower the resolution of the Roman army and people, it might become an intolerable drain on Rome's treasury, and eventually might result in a negotiated peace and the survival of Carthage.

In their camp near Utica, the exultant Roman consuls had every reason to be well pleased with their day's work. Since both nations loved peace—Carthage at any price, and Rome in her own fashion, provided she gained all her objectives—the Romans could justifiably congratulate themselves that the negotiations were a huge success. It would be difficult for any future cold war to equal Rome's winnings in the one just ended. All that remained to be done was to gather the spoils of this bloodless victory.

The consuls, however, could not forget the hysterical outburst of anger when the delegates heard the death sentence for their city. Probably the same thing would happen in Carthage when the delegates reported. So the consuls decided on prudence. On the assumption that the Carthaginians would soon forget their anger and become submissive again, they would grant Carthage a cooling-off period; then they would camp their legions under the city walls, sail their fleet into the harbors, and turn the city over to plunder and destruction. After all, this had been the promise held out to recruits for Rome's expeditionary force: booty without death or wounds.

The Roman consuls had no doubts, no premonition of trouble. Had they not the precedent of 238 B.C. when their country had declared war against a helpless Carthage, a war that had never been fought but had brought them endless gains? What matter if the world would deem this new act of ruthless exploitation equally shameful? An additional stain on her record was a small price for Rome to pay for securing her southern flank. Too bad the Roman soothsayers did not foresee that on this same southern flank a grandson of King Masinissa would lead his Numidians in a bloody war against Rome a generation later.

For the aggressors, the first and great surprise was the declaration of war; but more surprises were to come. The Roman consuls had expected soon to see the Carthaginians emerging as refugees from the city gates, carrying what they could, seeking a new home ten miles from the sea. Instead they found these unpredictable Carthaginians manning their walls, now ready to die to preserve the freedom they had been willing to surrender only a few days earlier.

It was a war of a faceless people, of an anonymous crowd, without a single celebrated hero in the three years' resistance. Even the brave woman, the wife of the last general who surrendered, who threw herself and her children into the flames to avoid Roman captivity, is known only as Hasdrubal's wife—a heroine without a name.

To support her armies in Spain and against Carthage in 149, Rome had a population far larger than that of Carthage, whose people within the city walls numbered between 150,000 and 200,000, with probably another 500,000 outside the walls. Within the walls, her maximum mobilizable force fit for military duty never exceeded 30,000 men.

Carthage's walls would be a serious obstacle to attack. The twenty miles of fortifications were among the strongest in the ancient world. Moreover, at that time well-designed masonry fortifications were stronger than offensive weapons. Yet, the strongest walls cannot ward off aggression unless they are manned by defenders of courage and endurance, armed with good weapons.

XI

CARTHAGE PREPARES
FOR WAR

The morning after declaring war, Carthage awoke before dawn. There was so much to be done, and so little time. As quickly as possible the Carthaginians must transform their declaration of war from a mere gesture of defiance into a viable defense. Arms and the men—these were the problems. It no doubt fell to Hasdrubal Numidianus to select the men for the army, assign them to appropriate sectors on the walls, and take all other steps to prepare for the Roman assault.

Fortunately Carthage had hundreds of skilled artisans, usually employed in the arsenal and the shipyards, who could supervise the untrained men and women who flocked to answer the call for workers to manufacture weapons. The first industrial mobilization for war of which a record is available was on its way. Appian describes it in this fashion:

All the sacred places, the temples, and every other wide and open space, were turned into workshops, where men and women worked together day and night, on a fixed schedule, without pause, eating by turns. Each day they made 100 shields, 300 swords, 1,000 missiles for catapults, 500 javelins and spears, and as many catapults as they could. For the torsion ropes to fire them, the women cut off their hair for want of other fibers.

The city's furnaces and forges, by the hundreds, each small, with only a few employees, worked hard to produce the metal parts of weapons and shields and helmets. Woodworkers made the shafts for spears and the frames and other wooden parts for catapults.

Catapults were the light, medium, and heavy artillery of ancient and medieval warfare, and at the time of the Third Punic War had been used for some three hundred years. A development of the bow and arrow, the catapult consisted of a gun carriage of heavy beams, elastic ropes tightened to high tension by a windlass, and a trigger mechanism. It hurled heavy arrows in direct fire, and round stone or concrete projectiles weighing as much as 60 pounds, in curved fire; it attained excellent accuracy up to 200 yards and had a maximum range of 500 yards. The ropes were made of sinews, horsehair, or women's hair and required frequent replacement because of the loss of elasticity. Women's hair served best, and patriotic women in the ancient world proudly sacrificed their prized tresses in the service of their countries. Polybius tells of a king who shipped several tons of hair to Rhodes for the island's defense, and the Roman historian Vegetius writes:

Once in a siege of the Capitol, when these weapons became unserviceable by long continued firing and when sinews were all used up, Roman matrons cut off their hair to send to their husbands in battle. The artillery was restored to service; the attack was repulsed. These most virtuous women preferred a life of freedom with their husbands, even with their beauty lost for a time, than with their beauty intact to become slaves to the enemy.

The women of Carthage showed equal fortitude and devotion, and the catapult played an important part in Carthage's defense. The catapult was used almost exclusively in attack and defense of permanent fortifications: since catapults weighed from 100 to 600 pounds, they were ill-adapted to mobile warfare and rarely were put to service in it. In defense, they occupied fixed positions on city walls and towers, in attack they were moved on rollers over leveled ground.

No record exists of the early military preparations made within Carthage. Appian merely refers to the "haste and zeal" the Carthaginians displayed in mobilizing for war. Without benefit of any evidence other than the successful repulse of the first Roman assault of the city walls a short time later, it is possible to infer the first steps Hasdrubal Numidianus took.

That night he probably slept, if at all, only a few hours. His first problem was to gather a staff. Next he would look to the remnants of the Sacred Band, so cruelly mauled in the Oroscopa campaign, to provide aides, mounted patrols, and messengers to carry orders to the commanders of the defensive sectors. He would order the patrols to ride at daylight to the high ground that concealed the Roman army and navy from Carthage, and establish observation outposts. Having provided for security, he next faced the problem of obtaining intelligence about enemy plans with infantry patrols and spies. He would establish communication with the other Hasdrubal concerning war plans and coordination.

The logical location of his headquarters was in one of the high towers of the powerful citadel walls on the Byrsa. It was centrally situated; it looked out on most of the city's defenses and on a large part of what was left of the Carthaginian empire.

Shortly before dawn these preliminary steps would be completed. A brief pause for breakfast was in order. The general would mount to the top of the tower to see for himself if anything was happening in the direction of Utica. If the Romans moved on Carthage that day, there was little he could do to keep the enemy from scaling the walls. He prayed the gods for time. He was happy to see that nothing stirred on the Utica road; and soon reports from his patrols assured him that there was no movement yet from the Roman camp.

Pondering the probable actions of the enemy, he glanced eastward over the sparkling blue waters of the Gulf of Tunis to the long, high mountain on Cape Bon. The sun had just risen above this mountain, behind which were the country estates and fertile fields of wealthy Carthaginians and the farms of Libyan peasants. From them would come food for the people and his garrison. To the southeast, and a little nearer, rose the majestic heights of the two-horned mountain lying close to the waters of the gulf. Behind that mountain, in a strong defensive position, the other Hasdrubal blocked a Roman move by land to the Cape Bon peninsula. Hasdrubal Numidianus discussed the situation with his staff, and then surveyed the city itself. Directly below him on the strongly fortified acropolis was the enclosure of the temple of Eshmoun (Aesculapius in Greek).

He could see too the six-story apartment houses crowded around the foot of the Byrsa. He could see the forum with its government buildings close by the commercial harbor and the navy yard, which were strongly defended by their own circuit of walls. And to the north, in the direction of Cape Carthage, the heavily populated city gave way slowly to the scattered palaces and gardens of the wealthiest citizens in the area called the Megara. He looked on the beautiful city, the product of centuries of loving care, and found it a place well worth fighting for, and dying for if need be. In Hasdrubal Numidianus, Carthage had a general who knew how to defend the city and how to counterattack effectively when opportunity offered.

Carthage's twenty miles of fortifications were strongest where the ground most facilitated enemy attack. The isthmus leading to the city most needed powerful defenses, and here the engineers had built an impregnable fortification. Across the narrowest part of the isthmus lay a triple defense line, two to two and a half miles in length. Until recently its location was a matter of debate. But a French commander in Tunis, General R. Duval, flew over the area one day in 1949 when the light was favorable and noticed a light-colored streak across the isthmus. Excavation uncovered what may well be the outer moat, about sixty feet wide, back of which was a band of rock or concrete with regularly spaced holes. In the holes were the bottom sections of what may be the evidence that this is actually a part of the long-sought triple defense line. For in his treatise on Fortification, Philo of Byzantium, who wrote in the second century B.C., describes obstacles designed to prevent the enemy from rolling up the heavy siege devices, such as battering rams and movable towers. He recommended that large excavations should be dug, deep enough to bury parallel lines of tall, empty amphorae, standing upright. The holes in the rock found by General Duval would keep the earthen jars in that position. "The necks of the amphorae," Philo writes, "should be closed with moss to prevent the empty, hollow jars from giving off a sound [when the enemy probed with long poles to discover such obstacles]. Afterward they are covered with earth to allow men to walk over the ground without risk; but in such a way that under the weight of siege engines, the ground gives away."

General Duval's discovery places this front about two and a half miles from the acropolis on the Byrsa. This line, however, extends only about two miles from the Lake of Tunis. This may be explained by the greater area of the lagoon of Ariana in antiquity. Behind the moat stood the outer wall, lower than the main wall which rose to a height of 45 feet, with battlements and with towers every 200 feet. The towers were four stories high and, with a depth of 30 feet, provided, with their catapults, excellent flanking fire if the enemy ever approached the wall with battering rams. But on the triple-defense lines of Carthage this never happened. The inner and stronger wall was divided into two stories. In the lower there were stables for 300 elephants, with storage space for their feed. In the upper, reached by ramps, were stables for 4,000 horses with space for their fodder. There were barracks also for soldiers, 20,000 foot and 4,000 horse. The remainder of the defense line around the city was a single wall with towers at intervals for flanking the curtain walls and the gates leading to the exterior.

No trace of this single wall has been found because when the Romans tore down the walls, after the war, builders quarried the heavy blocks of stone. But the story of the siege supplies enough information to permit placing most sections of the wall with reasonable accuracy. For instance, Appian reports that the wall running from the western end of the strong defenses on the peninsula along the Lake of Tunis to the entrance of the harbor "was the only weak and low spot in the fortifications, having been neglected from the beginning." Perhaps Appian means "weak" only in comparison with the triple-defense line.

This outer defense line did not by any means end the city's capacity to resist. The citadel which is called "the strongest part of the city" and the ports had their own defenses. The citadel hill, the Byrsa, 160 feet above sea level, had a massive wall of masonry about a half mile in length around the summit of the hill.

Carthage had also fortified the commercial harbor and the naval base with a double-defense wall of considerable strength. These walls not only protected the naval base; they also prevented anyone from observing the number and type of naval vessels or any activity in the harbor.

The two harbors for commerce and defense are particularly interesting because of their role in the siege, and because they still exist, in a shrunken state, the sole reminders of the trade and naval power of the one-time Queen of the Western Mediterranean. These ports were carefully designed for their special functions. They had been excavated and some of the paved bottom is still in place. The Carthaginians called these man-made harbors *cothons*, which means "dug out." An entrance to the harbor, 70 feet wide, opened into the small bay of Kram, facing south. Iron chains closed this entrance in time of war.

The commercial harbor was rectangular with sufficient length to enable freighters to tie up for loading and unloading cargo. Warships had to pass through the commercial harbor and a protected channel to enter the naval base, which was circular. In the center of the circle was, and still is, a small circular island on which, in ancient times, stood a tower to house the admiral commanding the fleet. The tower was higher than the nearby sea wall of the city, to enable the admiral to observe what was going on at sea. From his headquarters his trumpeters and heralds could give signals and call out orders to his ship captains to ensure orderly entrance and exit of the warships. On the perimeter of the island and on the opposite circuit of the port were 220 radial slips, possibly roofed, to house the fleet. Two Ionic columns stood in front of each slip to give the appearance of a continuous portico to both the harbor and island.

The dimensions of the harbor today are undoubtedly much smaller than formerly, but probably never more than two or three warships could be afloat in it at the same time. Putting to sea must have required careful control from the admiral's command post which had to function like a modern airfield control tower.

M. Pierre Cintas, the erudite French archaeologist and authority on Carthage, has advanced a convincing hypothesis to explain how these ports of such small dimensions functioned. He sees a close analogy between the handling of ships in port two thousand years ago and airplane traffic today. The ancient mariners took their ships into some port every night, when possible, to feed and rest their crews and to take care of the hulls. Ships were small, living space cramped, navigation at night difficult. A day's travel averaged about twenty-five miles. Ordinarily the landing place was a beach, on an island, or close to the mouth of a river, on which the ships, ordinarily not longer than a hundred feet with a draft of three or four feet, could be hauled ashore. Like today's airplanes and their operating personnel, the ships and crews required terra firma and shelter for daily maintenance and rest at the end of the trip. Consequently, both natural and artificial Punic harbors, like the cothon at Carthage, needed only the limited space to float ships long enough to enable the landing details to haul them ashore or into their slips. The famous Punic island-city of Motya off the western coast of Sicily had a cothon even smaller than the one at Carthage, as I was able to verify during two airplane flights over the island in 1960.

Some time before the Third Punic War, the interior commercial harbor became too limited in size for larger merchant vessels and increased trade. Carthage built a long and spacious wharf against the city wall, extending southward as a breakwater for ships entering the old harbor.

The enormous submerged blocks of stone in this area confirm Appian's account of this construction which plays an essential role in the siege. For this breakwater-pier Appian uses the Greek word *chōma*, which means a mole or pier carried out into the sea. Use of this mole for unloading freighters on the landward side would seem to have been not only feasible, but essential by the end of the Second Punic War. Cargo ships had been growing larger to carry upward of 300 tons. Such merchantmen would have found it difficult if not impossible to maneuver in the cramped space of the old commercial harbor. Furthermore, when the volume of trade increased, as it clearly did after the Second Punic War, Carthaginian carriers doubtless transported iron and tin to Egypt which under the Ptolemies became the center of commerce in the eastern Mediterranean. Such a wharf had become indispensable.

This was the situation and the physical appearance of Carthage as the people labored mightily to meet the ordeal by armed conflict.

XII

MONTH OF CARTHAGINIAN
VICTORIES

The two Roman consuls in Utica discussed with amazement the news that the unpredictable Carthaginians had declared war. Of course, there was no reason to worry, or even to hasten the advance to Carthage. Give these hysterical merchants, mariners, and priests a few days to come to their senses. Judging by the years of appeasement, these people had no stomach for fighting. As soon as they saw the Roman fleet sailing past their ramparts and covering the Lake of Tunis with a force able to blockade their harbors and to starve them into submission—as soon as they observed the legions concentrating in front of their defenses, blocking land traffic into the city, and ready to attack, they would recognize the folly of fighting.

So, without worry, the consuls lingered near Utica. Appian suggests that they delayed their advance perhaps because "they hesitated about performing such an atrocious act [as wiping out Carthage] . . . and besides, they thought they could capture an unarmed city by storm whenever they liked."

It was not so simple as that. The Romans were unprepared for this resistance. Supplies were running short. Even the surrender of additional Carthaginian cities had not brought in food enough to supply the Roman forces. And Hasdrubal's army outside the walls was keeping the Romans away from the richest agricultural area of

the country. Perhaps the Romans would have to requisition supplies from Italy or Sicily. Furthermore, although the consuls were
fairly certain there would be little or no effective resistance, an
early assault would necessitate the building of scaling ladders and
the collection of material for filling the deep ditch on the isthmian
front, the only approach by land.

Roman war aims were uncomplicated: Occupy Carthage, drive
out the population, destroy the city, and put a curse on the land
to prevent anyone from building another commercial and naval
base on this ideal site for control of the narrows between North
Africa and Sicily.

Strategically, the Roman consuls planned to seize and keep the
initiative, move on Carthage, and use terror to win the war without
fighting. If Carthage refused to surrender, capture the city by immediate assault. Presumably their plans called for the occupation
of Tunis too, for the road to Hasdrubal's army outside the walls
led through that city and the position was too important to be left
unoccupied.

Carthage was forced by circumstances to remain on the defensive.
Mobilization, military and industrial, had just begun. At all costs
the Carthaginians must avoid pitched battle; Roman superiority
in numbers and weapons would make defeat certain. They would
count on the walls and on Hasdrubal's army in the field, which
enjoyed notable geographic and tactical advantages.

The Carthaginian war aim, for the moment at least, was clear.
Hasdrubal Numidianus must make the city secure. He must prepare a defense that would prolong the siege until the Romans, with
reduced morale and with the cost of siege warfare becoming un-
endurable, would offer acceptable peace terms. Hasdrubal's mission
was more active: by guerrilla warfare he would (1) prevent or
hamper Roman foraging; (2) safeguard the Carthaginian food
supply; and (3) threaten raids on the main Roman army. Since
effective naval blockade was almost impossible with the warships
of that epoch, and since the few miles from Cape Bon to Car-

thage could be easily traveled by blockade runners at night, Hasdrubal would prevent famine in the city.

One other pressing problem confronted the Roman consuls before their departure from Utica. Could they depend on Masinissa? So far they had ignored their old ally, who had fought for decades to diminish Carthaginian power. Of course he had reaped the harvest of his labors. Numidia was now a strong and united kingdom with cities built, no doubt, by hired Carthaginian architects and engineers. But Masinissa might imperil the Roman objective, if the consuls further alienated him.

Moreover, the consuls had certainly heard that a grandson of Masinissa now commanded in Carthage. Consequently, they must change the policy of aloofness toward Masinissa, which undoubtedly had been decided upon by the Senate before they left Rome. True, they could probably count on the old man's early death and the succession to power of three legitimate sons— there were said to be forty-four others—so Numidia might soon be easier to handle.

Accordingly the consuls sent word to him that they would welcome Numidian assistance. Irritated by their cavalier treatment, Masinissa answered that he would send aid to the Romans

whenever he should see that they needed it. Not long after he sent to inquire if they wanted anything at present. They, not tolerating his haughtiness and already suspicious of him as a disaffected person, answered that they would send for him whenever they needed him.

Perhaps the Carthaginians' appointment of his grandson to command in Carthage was, after all, a stroke of political genius.

Less than a week after the declaration of war, the consuls held a final review and inspection of their legions and fleet before moving against their main objective. They had every reason to believe that the end would come quickly, although they would need two or three days to concentrate the army and navy under the walls of

Carthage. The distance from their camp to Carthage was short, but the single road crossed the Medjerda River on a bridge and a high hill before reaching Ariana. Moreover, 84,000 men on the march stretched out many miles. Even if half the army embarked on the transports at Utica, leaving the other 40,000 or so men to take the overland route, at least two days would be necessary to assemble the forces at Carthage. So far, they had no idea how the Carthaginians were profiting by the Roman delay.

After Manilius, in command of the army, had reached the highest point of the road from Utica via Ariana, the city of Carthage on its peninsula came in sight. Manilius saw the miles of formidable walls, the strongly fortified citadel and the temple on the Byrsa dominating the tall buildings. He could see the road from Carthage to Tunis athwart which he planned to camp. The naval commander, Censorinus, proposed to establish his camp not far from the outer ditch of the city's isthmian defenses, on the Lake of Tunis itself, so that the warships not on guard duty and drawn up on shore could be enclosed in the perimeter of its defenses.

When the consuls arrived, they looked for a delegation under a flag of truce offering to surrender the city. Instead, they saw the city walls crowded with armed soldiers. Their war plan had been prepared for what they were convinced would be a most unlikely contingency: it called for an assault launched simultaneously on two widely separated fronts, a pincer movement that could not fail. If such an attack became necessary, another week would pass before they could move. To cover the assault with artillery fire, they would have to bring up from Utica the catapults the Carthaginians had surrendered.

On a morning early in May, 149 B.C., the Carthaginian outposts on the high ground between their city and Utica reported the Roman army and navy on the move. Hasdrubal Numidianus thanked the gods for the delay in the enemy's advance. Each day had increased the number of defenders and weapons, and had seen improvement in training and morale. Already some catapults and their ammunition were mounted on the more important towers, and the garrison assigned to the walls where they anticipated the first assault had carried up fire pots to drop on the enemy and his scaling ladders, and forked poles to push the ladders away from the wall. Nevertheless, against so powerful a foe, Carthaginians could hardly help feeling nervous.

During the afternoon the defenders on the isthmian front saw the Roman advance guard drawing near. It halted at some distance from the outer ditch. The rest of the column slowly advanced and spread out on each side of the road. Following the Roman custom, they started to fortify their camp.

Hasdrubal Numidianus had also observed their approach from his command post on the acropolis. Almost simultaneously he could see the Roman fleet rounding the headland at Cape Carthage. Soon the waters in front of the city's sea wall were crowded with the warships, supply vessels, and transports heading for the Lake of Tunis. It was not a sight to encourage optimism in Carthage.

Near the end of the second week since Carthage had declared war, the consuls completed preparations for the first assault. They had finished filling a section of the dry moat, sixty feet wide and twenty feet deep, to enable them to advance on a front sufficient to ensure success.

A barrage of arrows from a contingent of Rome's auxiliary troops kept the Carthaginian defenders on the outer wall under cover, and the Romans occupied it without too much trouble. Ahead stood the main defense line, a wall forty-five feet high, with flanking towers every two hundred feet. A multitude of well-armed defenders, shouting insults and using arrows and javelins, killed or wounded many of the legionaries approaching with heavy scaling ladders whose length the engineers had calculated after estimating the height of the wall. The Roman soldiers were grateful for the support by catapult missiles aimed at the tops of the walls and towers. Meanwhile, naturally, the attackers feinted at other points.

As Manilius directed the attack on the isthmian defenses, Censorinus, five miles away, undertook an even more difficult assault. He led an amphibious operation against the single wall, of lesser height, that ran near and, frequently, immediately at the edge of the Lake of Tunis. This was the southern front of the Carthaginians' defense line, which they had not fortified so elaborately. The reason was plain. The lake served as a moat; battering rams and movable towers could approach the wall only if mounted on ships, and then only with great difficulty because of shallow water and the weight of the devices. Where there was land enough at the foot of the wall, Censorinus raised ladders from the ground. Where ships could approach close to the foot of the wall, he used another siege device well known in Greek and Roman warfare.

Polybius describes this type of war machine in reporting the Roman attack on Syracuse in the Second Punic War in 215 B.C. It was a massive scaling ladder called a *sambuca*, from the Greek word for a triangular musical instrument with four strings. This device required two quinquiremes lashed together to provide a base. The outside oars of this combination would row it close to the wall to be assaulted. The ladder, four feet wide and long enough to reach the top of the wall, lay fore and aft along the deck, extending beyond the bows, until ropes and pulleys supported on the masts of the galleys raised it against the wall. Ample protection on the sides and at the top of the ladder was provided for the manning detail.

But superiority in manpower and machinery was not enough. The Carthaginians fought courageously, and Appian reports that the Romans "were astounded and retreated. Thus they met a rebuff at the very beginning, in expecting to take the city without fighting."

This first engagement of the Third Punic War was a resounding victory for Carthage. The Romans, however, were not daunted. They analyzed their defeat. They would try again, correcting any tactical errors made in their first attempt.

The second assault, made in much the same manner as the first, had a similar ending. "The spirits of the Carthaginians were very much raised" by these two victories, Appian reports. The consuls called a staff conference. The fleet would continue its day-and-night vigil, of course, and ultimately a naval blockade would reduce the city by famine. But that would take a long time. They would have to supplement the catapults that Carthage had turned over a few weeks earlier, and they would have to build more ladders for a third attempt to scale the walls. But the consuls saw also that their engineers would have to design and build better and different offensive weapons.

Ancient armies depended on engineer detachments to build catapults and battering rams on the spot, for such siege engines were too heavy for transport with an army in the field. Certain mechanical parts could be carried in the supply column, but the timber for the machines had to be cut and assembled when the need arose. Since the consuls required many more scaling ladders and since the new tactical plan called for two giant battering rams, the Big Berthas of their time, with their protective and supporting sheds, suitable timber must be obtained in large quantities.

Forests across the Lake of Tunis offered the most convenient supply. Timber cut there could readily be shipped by water or floated almost to the point where the woodworkers waited. This time the Roman army would redeem its reputation by breaking down enough of the walls to enable the legions to enter the city.

There was, however, one difficulty in carrying out this plan. Not only had Carthaginian morale been raised to a high pitch by two victories, but Carthaginian strength had increased amazingly; the city's defense force had quickly attained its maximum of 30,000 men, and Hasdrubal, outside the walls, had another 30,000 men. His strongly fortified camp was admirably located for all his

114

missions. It was about twenty miles from Carthage, a few miles from the town of Nepheris which Strabo describes as "a city fortified by nature and built upon a rock." From his camp, his army constantly threatened Roman security. With the aid of the mountainous terrain and the road through a narrow pass, even his comparatively small force could protect the Cape Bon peninsula from Roman depredation or foraging. It was only a few miles from the forests where the Romans would go for timber. These were its strategic advantages.

With Hasdrubal hovering on their rear, the consuls felt obliged to strengthen materially the defenses of their camps. That took time. Every day the Romans devoted to fortifying their camps was another day Carthage used to increase its armament and to train recruits.

When at length his field fortifications seemed satisfactory, Censorinus crossed the lake in his transports in search of timber. The legionaries assigned to fell trees and cut beams and planks set to work. The tallest and straightest trees would serve to make the battering rams, but the Romans needed lumber also to build a corduroy road to the rams' emplacement platforms, and sheds to protect the rams and their crews.

Aware of Hasdrubal's proximity, Censorinus had posted guards around the working area. But they were either too few, or too close to the working parties, or napping. Shouting terrifying battle cries, Carthaginian cavalry burst without warning from the woods encircling the Roman soldiers, most of whom had stacked their arms in order to work. When the raid had ended, the Romans counted about five hundred casualties and the loss of many valuable tools. And thus, in less than a month since her declaration of war, Carthage had won three victories, Rome had suffered three humiliating defeats.

In this fashion "the Carthaginian cavalry general Himilco, surnamed Phameas," entered the scene. Unlike most of his countrymen, he had two names, but history refers to him usually as

Phameas. In his daring cavalry tactics, in his effective way of doing the unexpected, he was an eminent precursor of Jeb Stuart.
Until his life took a turn as surprising as his tactics, he made the
Romans fear and respect him as they feared no other Carthaginian
general in the Third Punic War.

Several weeks, perhaps more, would be needed to complete the
rams and fill in the area below the wall where they would be
placed. The Roman army could not afford to be idle that long.
So in spite of poor morale, lowered by Phameas's raid and the
two failures to storm the walls, Manilius and Censorinus ordered
a third coordinated assault on the city. It too failed.

Censorinus now devoted all his manpower to preparing the two
battering rams. Attack over the walls could not succeed; an attack
that breached the walls could not fail. Manilius also decided to
wait. Although he had destroyed sections of the advanced wall,
he despaired of further assaults on the impregnable isthmian front.
The Roman army sat down to await the completion of the siege
engines and the preparation of the terrain.

Since the outbreak of the Third Punic War, only one month
had elapsed. But the Carthage that used to be had disappeared
forever. The four victories the Carthaginians had won inspired
growing hope—even confidence—in a successful outcome of the
war.

XIII

MORE ROMAN DEFEATS

June of 149 B.C. began in Carthage amid relative calm. Roman attempts to storm the walls had ceased. But within the city, the people toiled unflaggingly to provide weapons for the army, which took no rest in its training and tactical maneuvers. The soldiers knew that the inevitable sequel to the enemy's futile efforts to scale the walls would be the use of the battering ram to make a ground-level passage through the wall into the city. And soon Hasdrubal Numidianus saw where the Romans planned to make their next main attack.

For some time, the Carthaginians on the wall skirting the Lake of Tunis had observed increasing Roman activity along the Taenia, the sand spit separating the lake from the gulf. There was at least one channel through the Taenia so that ships could enter the Lake of Tunis. A German archaeologist, R. Oehler by name, has suggested on the basis of Appian's descriptions that Carthage had excavated a second channel at the foot of the city wall through the sandy barrier. He argues, plausibly enough, that Appian's description of the earth-moving and filling operation to enlarge the contracted space at the end of the sand spit near the city applies equally well under his hypothesis. Such a channel would have provided a moat at least sixty feet wide, adding greatly to the defensive strength of this sector.

The Roman plans for the next phase of the siege necessitated widening of the Taenia where it adjoined the city wall but only if long-range missiles kept the Carthaginians under cover could this work proceed. We must accordingly imagine a line of catapults about two hundred yards from the Carthaginian wall, and a body of archers and slingers from the auxiliaries at half that range, on the alert to smother any attempt to harass the labor details. In front of and behind these defenders, thousands of men under Censorinus dumped loads of earth and stone alongside the Taenia near the city; two long sheds and two battering rams of unusual length and diameter also began to take shape.

The Carthaginians knew exactly what countermeasures to take. They were well versed in the art of siegecraft. From long experience, they knew all the devices for the attack and defense of cities. They were well aware that many a city had been lost through subversion facilitated by bitter factional disunity within the city. History, however, records no traitor in the city of Carthage during the siege; the pro-Roman party, by this time, must have withered in numbers and influence following Rome's criminal assault on the city. There was little to fear from this faction. The danger from internal treachery in those centuries, however, existed to such a degree that the military manual of Aeneas Tacticus, written about 360 B.C., describes at great length the ways to circumvent it.

An ancient siege, as was manifest in the previous month, against a weakly held city, began with an attempt to storm the walls. If these attacks failed, battering rams would be the next step in the offensive of a besieging army. If they were found to be ineffective, the besieger might surround the walls with a trench line plus a naval blockade of a city on the sea coast, to starve the inhabitants into submission. A more aggressive general might try to save time by tunneling and undermining walls and towers or by building huge ramps and mounds to bring up high wooden towers mounted on rollers to overtop the defenses of the city. The Romans did neither at Carthage.

The Roman army's reputation for its engineering achievements unquestionably increased an enemy's dread of its siege operations.

118

The habit of fortifying a camp after each day's march put the spade in the hands of Roman soldiers far more often than the sword. But the morale of the disillusioned legionaries, expecting only a short walk in the sun before plundering Carthage, most certainly fell to a low ebb while this month of hard labor continued. The battering rams, they hoped, would open the road to victory and loot.

A battering ram was a wooden beam or tree trunk, sometimes as much as 180 feet long, with a bronze or iron head. Such a ram, with a diameter of 28 inches, would weigh about twenty tons. Leather thongs were fastened along the beam for the use of the manning detail, which might number many hundreds of men on each shift. The ram approached the city walls under a massive steep-roofed shed, called a tortoise or turtle, which moved forward on rollers. As Vegetius explains it, "A testudo or tortoise takes its name from its likeness to a live tortoise. Just as the turtle withdraws its head and thrusts it out, so the battering ram is pulled back as far as possible and then driven forward by the manning detail so that it may strike with greater force." The shed had two functions. It had to be strong enough to resist or deflect falling stones or fire-tipped missiles from the walls, and its roof and sides were covered with hides to prevent fires. The shed also served to support the ram by means of chains from the central roof beam.

The defenders, letting down a noose, attempted to grapple the head of the ram as it emerged in its forward thrust. They also let down soft mattresses to absorb the ram's blows. If the wall showed signs of collapsing, the defenders built a short crescent-shaped wall behind it.

When Censorinus completed his preparations the area at the end of the Taenia had been widened for the two battering rams under their protecting sheds, and for additional smaller sheds for the legionaries assigned to attack through the expected breach. Although each blow of a battering ram of the size built to attack the Carthaginian wall was the equivalent of only a small-caliber modern projectile, the long-continued blows on the same area ultimately broke through the strongest masonry.

Six thousand men were assigned to each ram, and to roll these siege engines close to the wall required the entire crew. When the breaching operation began, however, the manning detail was divided into many reliefs, which took turns at swinging the ram back and forth. It was essential that there be no interruption until the wall gave way. To heighten enthusiasm for the task, Censorinus fostered rivalry between the two crews. One team consisted of legionaries commanded by military tribunes; the other six thousand were sailors commanded by ships' captains. Which would break through the wall first?

History does not record how long the battering rams took to breach the wall. But the Romans finally "beat down a part of the wall, so that they could look into the city. But even so the Carthaginians drove them back and began to repair the breach in the wall by night."

When it became clear to the Carthaginians that the damage was too extensive to be repaired that night, and that the wet mortar between the blocks of stone they had replaced would not dry by morning, they made a quick and courageous decision. They decided on an immediate night attack. The manual of Aeneas Tacticus laid down rules for organizing secret sallies by night; their training during the two months since mobilization paid off. The Carthaginians "rushed out some men armed and others only carrying torches, to set fire to the rams and sheds. They had not time to burn these entirely, because the Romans ran up to prevent them, but they made them quite unserviceable and regained the city."

Daylight showed the breach to be still wide enough to enable troops to pass, and the Romans could see beyond the gap an open space in which they could maneuver and fight. They organized their attack. Carthaginian troops crowded on the roofs of neighboring houses and formed dense lines of infantry in a semicircle from wall to wall on the ground. They surrounded and drove back the Romans who entered the city, in what might easily have proved a Roman disaster.

But a brilliant young Roman staff officer intervened at the psychological moment. He was the same staff officer who had witnessed the battle from the heights between Hasdrubal and Masinissa in 150 B.C. Scipio, to be called a few years later Scipio Africanus the Younger, had seen the danger to the Roman advance across the breach. On his own initiative, he had kept his men out of the fray and ordered them to mount the walls on each side of the breach. The attacking force, hemmed in on their front and flanks, retired in confusion, but Scipio prevented a catastrophic pursuit. "And this action first brought him renown, as he had shown himself wiser than the general," Appian wrote.

At this point, history gives us the one specific date in the year 149 B.C. which suggests a reasonable chronology for the year's events. Appian reports: "Now the dog star began to rise and sickness broke out in the army of Censorinus, whose camp was pitched on a lake of stagnant and impure water, under high walls shutting off the fresh breezes from the sea." The Dog Star, Sirius, rises on July 26 and heralds the scorching heat of the dog days. Censorinus shifted his camp to the Taenia, where his men enjoyed the fresh air from the gulf. His fleet also left the malodorous waters of the lake and beached, when not on blockade duty, along the gulf shore within his defenses.

The Roman redeployment enabled Carthage's defenders to move against the Roman navy. Appian writes:

The Carthaginians, whenever the wind blew toward the Romans, hauled small boats, filled with twigs and tow, under the walls [of their sea-front], where they could not be seen by the enemy. When they were turning the corner, and were just about to be sighted, they poured sulfur and pitch over the contents, spread the sails, and as the wind filled them, set fire to the boats. These, driven by the wind and the fury of the flames against the Roman ships, set fire to them and came a little short of destroying the whole fleet.

The Carthaginians anticipated here the doctrine of Frederick the Great. To emphasize the value of surprise in war, he urged his generals to shift back and forth from the skin of the lion to the skin of the fox. Up to this time, Carthage had won by sheer bravery. Now it tried surprise. It succeeded admirably. Carthage will don the skin of the fox many times in the next two years. Their resistance from 149 to 146 B.C. proves how powerful is surprise among the principles of strategy. Properly used, it is a source of decisive advantage in war.

Soon after this success, the Carthaginians felt strong enough to take the initiative on land. They had come a long way from the dispirited and apathetic appeasers of a few months earlier. They planned a surprise attack on the camp which Manilius had fortified for his army on the isthmus, probably not more than four hundred yards from the Carthaginian defense line. A detachment of armed men, accompanied by crews carrying planks to bridge the Roman ditch, charged the enemy defenses. The surprise sally resulted in panicky confusion in the Roman camp, which ended only when Scipio led out cavalry from the rear gates and frightened the Carthaginians into retirement within their walls. Thus, a second time Scipio by bold initiative saved the Roman army.

Manilius alone now commanded the besiegers. Censorinus, "to conduct the election," had returned to Rome, doubtless happy to exchange his uniform for a toga.

An army of only 30,000 men in Carthage had made its position unassailable by an army nearly three times its strength. The formidable barrier of the city's walls held against repeated and savage assaults by a defensive that was not passive but most active in attacking the investing troops.

No longer did the peace-loving Carthaginians fear struggle and conflict. In the beginning the Carthaginians may have resorted to violence and war because they preferred glorious suicide to a lingering death of an exiled population. But would hatred and anger prevail after the initial hysterical outburst? Or would calm reflection on Rome's crushing superiority on land and sea develop enough fear to bring about a second surrender? Now we know the answer. Anger and hatred and love of country and freedom aroused an indomitable will to resist. Now Carthaginians had an objective that unified factions and classes, a goal worth fighting and dying for. Their resistance combined the fanatical fervor of a religious crusade in defense of their gods and temples with the defense of their families and homes, of their way of life, of their very existence. These motives created a national morale, previously almost nonexistent. Each successive military victory raised their morale still further. Now hope strengthened morale.

Carthaginians could now look forward to the survival of their beloved city. No longer did they fear the Roman legions. They knew now that they could cope with the redoubtable enemy at their gates. Prolonged resistance would win a negotiated peace; Carthage would not be destroyed. Their city walls plus their unconquerable spirit would hold off the Roman army until war-weariness and the peace party in Rome would force a settlement. In the short space of a few months, Carthaginian morale had become the immovable body to what had seemed to be an irresistible force. In that time hopeful confidence in victory had replaced the forlorn hope of honorable self-destruction. So potent a force is morale in the strength of a nation.

XIV

ROME TRIES THE

INDIRECT APPROACH

As the Romans buried their dead and bound their wounds, they could find little cause for self-congratulation. Carthage had humiliated Rome as no nation had ever done before. The world and the expeditionary force remembered that a Roman army of 84,000 men and a strong fleet faced a cringing, peace-at-any-price people with only a stone wall between them and annihilation. And now the Romans knew and the world would soon know that for three months Carthage had beaten back every assault.

Manilius recognized that once more he would have to change the Roman strategy. The Carthaginians had proved effectively that they were more than willing and able to defeat the direct approach. Rome would turn to the indirect approach as a better, if not the only, way to victory.

Manilius had learned a lesson from the night attack on his camp. The first step was to strengthen his fortifications defending the camp. The near success of the enemy attack frightened him into replacing inadequate palisades with a wall and a ditch in front. Appian adds that he also strongly entrenched a second camp "where his supply ships came in," probably at Sebkret es Ariana. If we assume that the water was deep enough for shipping and that a channel to this lagoon existed two thousand years ago, we may locate there the new Roman camp. It would have saved

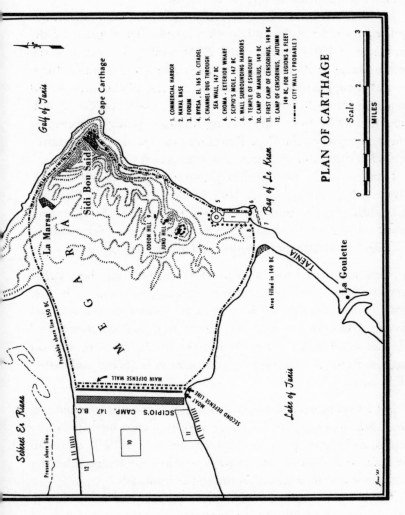

PLAN OF CARTHAGE

1. COMMERCIAL HARBOR
2. NAVAL BASE
3. FORUM
5. BYRSA - EL 165 ft. CITADEL
5. CHANNEL DUG THROUGH
   SEA WALL, 147 BC
6. CHOMA - EXTERIOR WHARF
7. SCIPIO'S MOLE, 147 BC
8. WALL SURROUNDING HARBORS
9. TEMPLE OF ESHMOUN?
10. CAMP OF MANILIUS, 149 BC
11. FIRST CAMP OF CENSORINUS, 149 BC
12. CAMP OF CENSORINUS, AUTUMN
    149 BC, FOR LEGIONS & FLEET
    ⋯⋯ CITY WALL (PROBABLE)

Scale

0   1   2   3
MILES

City of Carthage in the Third, or final, Punic War, 149–146 B.C. Probable locations of ports, defensive positions, and Roman siege works are shown. The war began with a siege, escalated into field operations, and ended in house-to-house combat, after which the city was razed.

many miles of travel for his supply ships, and would have provided within the fortifications beaching facilities for his warships, completely safe from another attack by fire.

Manilius continued the land and sea blockade of Carthage, but ordered no more costly and fruitless assaults. He organized a detachment of 10,000 infantry and 2,000 cavalry to march into the fertile Medjerda River valley and the countryside around Carthage to gather supplies. In the meantime the rest of the army would remain in camp to continue the blockade. Hasdrubal's army outside the walls, from their strong strategic position, prevented enemy foraging on the Cape Bon peninsula. Thanks to Hasdrubal's second in command, Phameas, that army served Carthage well.

Foraging parties under military tribunes, commanding in turn, ravaged the country. Hasdrubal's cavalry commander, Phameas, constantly pounced from ambush on these leaders who gave scant attention to security, causing serious losses to these detachments. Phameas, a master of guerrilla warfare, as Appian writes, was

a young and daring soldier, who had small but swift horses that lived on grass when they could find nothing else, and could bear both hunger and thirst when necessary—hiding in thickets and ravines, when he saw that the enemy were not on their guard [he] swooped down upon them from his hiding-place like an eagle, inflicted as much damage on them as he could, and darted away again.

But Phameas never attacked when Scipio was in command, because Scipio surrounded his foragers with a mixed infantry-cavalry screen, and personally rode constantly around the circle of guards with a mounted escort. He severely punished any forager who violated his orders to keep within the circle of outposts.

Appian's constant praise of Scipio is probably entirely deserved. Scipio unquestionably was an exceptional soldier, and a man of honor, who had been tutored by Polybius, who accompanied him in his final conquest of Carthage. Most of Polybius's eyewitness account of the Third Punic War has been lost but because the best part of Appian's history of Rome is his narrative of that war, there is general agreement that Appian has closely followed Polybius. In some measure this may explain the eulogistic references to Scipio, but later action of the Roman Senate and people testify independently to the admiration and high regard in which he was held.

He enjoyed the esteem of most of his countrymen, and was trusted as well by the enemy. Wealthy Carthaginians who owned country estates near the city found that when they surrendered to Scipio, they could rely on his promises to permit them to leave in safety, whereas other tribunes invariably violated the terms. Finally, such Carthaginians would make agreements only with Scipio.

Consequently, his fellow officers grew intensely jealous and spread rumors that Scipio had an understanding with the enemy because his family had enjoyed friendly relations with Carthaginians several generations earlier. One success gained by Scipio resulted in further disparagement by his rivals, but high praise elsewhere. It happened thus.

Sometime after the 12,000-man foraging detachment had returned to camp, Hasdrubal Numidianus undertook another nocturnal sally outside the city walls. Unaccountably, Carthaginians had not attacked while the Roman army was divided, for with Scipio absent, the chances for a successful raid would have been much greater.

The main Carthaginian objective was the newly fortified position by the Ariana lagoon, protecting the Roman ships. While citizens made all the din they could from the city walls to bewilder the enemy, Carthaginian soldiers rushed the two Roman camps, causing "tremendous confusion." Manilius, apparently fearing to go to the rescue of the naval camp, ordered his men to defend the walls of his own camp. But Scipio moved. He led ten troops of cavalry with lighted torches on a gallop around the assaulting force. He feinted advances and the Carthaginians broke formation and retreated into the city. Once again Scipio had saved the situation. Appian comments, "after all he had done, men talked of him as the only worthy successor of his father, Paulus, the conqueror of Macedonia, and of the Scipios into whose family he had been received by adoption."

Hasdrubal, with 30,000 men in camp only twenty miles away, did not take part in these two night attacks by the other Hasdrubal. A coordinated offensive, especially when Censorinus and his army were in camp on the Taenia, might have had more than a fair chance of success. But Hasdrubal outside the walls believed that his mission was purely defensive—a strategy which would seem sensible if he counted on Carthage to hold out against the successive Roman assaults, while acquiring strength and allies. In any event, his responsibility for safeguarding supplies for the city was of major importance. However, although avoiding pitched battle, Hasdrubal did send Phameas on his daring and effective raids, and Manilius decided that Hasdrubal's annoying and potentially dangerous army outside the walls must be destroyed.

During the staff conferences, Scipio advised strongly against Manilius's plan of attack. He pointed out that the road to the Carthaginian town of Nepheris, near which Hasdrubal's camp was located, ran through an easily defended pass, that the enemy camp was strongly entrenched, and that it stood atop a high hill difficult to attack. Scipio insisted that, to defeat Hasdrubal, catapults and other siege engines and a fortified camp for refuge in case of defeat were essential. An inexperienced general, Manilius refused to heed Scipio's objections. Since the end of his term of office was approaching, he may have felt that he had to move to save his reputation; if he defeated Hasdrubal, he might well finish off the war and win the coveted honor of a Roman triumph.

Hasdrubal held an ideal position. The steep approaches hampered assault, and a mountain stream—deep enough in the rainy season to require crossing only at fords—had cut a deep gully which served as a moat, dry or filled with water, to disrupt any advance to or withdrawal from the field of battle Hasdrubal had chosen. The stream curved advantageously around the front of Hasdrubal's camp, little more than a mile away from it. Only upstream, on Hasdrubal's left rear, was it easy to cross.

From this strong position, Phameas had raided enemy foraging parties with the success already noted. Strategically located on one of the two roads leading from Tunis to Cape Bon, it closed that road to an enemy advance. The other road to Cape Bon, winding around the foot of a lofty and forest-covered mountain with the gulf close to the flank of an army on the march, was only a few miles from the camp. It is interesting to note that even in our own time, this narrow passage continued to be a serious obstacle in the U.S. Army's campaign in Tunisia in World War II. *The U.S. Army in World War II: Northwest Africa* notes (p. 598) that in this area "the distance between steep heights and the surf on the Gulf of Tunis is only a few hundred yards. The coastal plain is thus readily defensible against an armored force by troops possessing the heights and equipped with appropriate weapons." *Plus ça change, plus c'est la même chôse.*

We do not know precisely the strength of the two armies that met in 149 B.C. on this most important battlefield of the Third Punic War, but Manilius probably had the superior force, even though he had necessarily left sufficient men in camp near Carthage for defense against an assault from the city.

Manilius presumably spent a night near Tunis, so that his army would cover the short distance to the battlefield in a few hours, and arrive in good condition to attack. Hasdrubal's army waited in a long line behind the bend in the stream and before their strongly fortified camp, a refuge if they had to retire.

This time Hasdrubal laid a trap instead of walking into one as he had done after Oroscopa. He might have decided to draw up his line of battle on his side of the stream. That would stopped the enemy, but would not have led to a victory. With the tactical cunning of a Hannibal, he stood far back from the stream, which the Romans would have to cross if they intended to fight.

Scipio, on arrival, immediately saw the danger and did his best to dissuade Manilius from his offensive. He pointed out deficiencies in Roman equipment—no artillery to attack Hasdrubal's camp, no material for filling up the gully. It was October, and since Appian mentions only a few fords across the stream, it may have been swollen by the autumn rains.

Scipio urged Manilius, if he persisted in his offensive, to fortify a camp to which the Romans could retreat if they were overpowered. Scipio evidently had little confidence in this army: its morale, after six months in Africa and a series of unsuccessful assaults on Carthage, must have been low. Its soldiers had looked forward to rich booty and no fighting. Instead, they often went hungry and hundreds of their comrades had been killed or wounded.

After the severe losses suffered in the previous months, it is unlikely that Manilius led more than 35,000 infantry to the battlefield. Each legion, with approximately 3,000 men in three lines, formed a front of three hundred yards. Hasdrubal, looking down from his position, estimated the Roman front with the legions in line at about a mile and a half long. He noted a cavalry force on the right flank of the Roman army, so, most probably, he ordered Phameas to a position opposite. Scipio commanded the enemy's mounted troops. Hasdrubal's inferiority in numbers—he never had more than 30,000 men—found compensation in the river and in the steep hill up which the enemy had to advance. His camp and the ravine at the foot of the hill would ensure the success of his plan.

Before coming within range of Carthaginian weapons, Manilius halted his army to rest and to restore its alignment, seriously upset in the unopposed crossing of the ravine. At last he gave the signal to attack. The trumpets sounded the charge. The centurions ordered double-time, but stopped the advance of cohorts about fifteen yards from the Carthaginians, to enable the front ranks, all along the line, to hurl their javelins. These men then fell back between cohorts and the whole front roared ahead wielding the short, two-edged swords so dreaded by Rome's enemies. The front-line soldiers cut and slashed and jabbed while the second line threw their javelins at the Carthaginians over the heads of the men whom they supported.

"There was great slaughter on both sides. Finally Hasdrubal withdrew into his heavily fortified camp, where he was safe and from which he could watch his chance of attacking the Romans as they moved off." Into these brief words, Appian compresses many hours of the first stage of the battle. What Phameas did, and how Hasdrubal withdrew through a few narrow gates into his camp are unrecorded. The withdrawal would have been difficult unless careful training for this very move had prepared the way. All we know is that Manilius by this time regretted his plan of battle: by now anyone could see the wisdom of Scipio's advice to build a camp for refuge in the event of a stalemate or defeat. Manilius had led his army into a trap from which only the most adept tactics could extricate it without severe loss. But Manilius lacked that kind of adeptness.

In the beginning of the next stage, Manilius seemed to be solving his problem. He ordered the surviving centurions to re-form the cohorts. He had marched up the hill; now he would march down, leaving Hasdrubal's army intact. Hasdrubal waited on the parapet of his camp for the moment when the Romans had broken ranks to ford the stream and their army was astride it, those who crossed being unable to support those still on the bank close to the enemy. Let Appian pick up the story:

When Hasdrubal saw [the Roman soldiers, in confusion and hardly moving] he made a more brilliant attack than ever, and slew a great number of them who fled without resistance. . . .

Scipio, taking 300 horsemen that he had with him and as many more as he could hastily collect, divided them into two bodies and led them, with many charges, against the enemy, by turns discharging darts at them and quickly retreating, then coming back at them and again quickly darting away, for he had given orders that one-half of them should advance by turns continually, discharge their javelins, and retire, as though they were attacking on all sides. This movement being constantly repeated without any intermission, the Africans, thus continuously assailed, turned against Scipio and pressed less heavily on those who were crossing. The latter thus had time to get across the stream, and then Scipio rode away after them under a shower of darts and with great difficulty.

At the beginning of this fight four Roman cohorts were cut off from the stream by the enemy and took refuge on a hill. These Hasdrubal surrounded, and the Romans did not miss them till they came to a halt. When they learned the facts they were in great perplexity. Some thought they ought to continue their retreat and not endanger the whole army for the sake of a few, but Scipio maintained that while deliberation was proper when you were laying your plans, yet in an emergency, when so many men and their standards were in danger, nothing but reckless daring was of any use. Then he himself, selecting some companies of horse, said that he would either rescue them or gladly perish with them. Taking two days' rations, he set out at once, the army being in great fear lest he should never return himself. When he came to the hill where the men were besieged he took possession of another eminence hard by and separated from the former by a narrow ravine. The Africans thereupon pressed the siege vigorously, making signals to each other and thinking that Scipio would not be able to relieve his friends after his forced march. But Scipio, seeing that the bases of the two hills curved around the ravine, lost no time, but dashed around them and secured a position above the enemy. They, finding themselves surrounded, fled in disorder. Scipio did not pursue them, as they were much superior in numbers.

Thus Scipio saved these men also, who had been given up for lost. When the army at a distance saw him returning safe himself, and having saved the others contrary to expectation, they shouted for joy and conceived the idea that he was aided by the same deity that was supposed to have enabled his grandfather Scipio to foresee the future.

In his enthusiasm for Scipio, Appian allocated to the most important pitched battle of the war less than one-third the space he took to describe Scipio's rescue of the four Roman cohorts. Many things we should like to know—for example, the role of Phameas at the height of the battle—remain unrecorded.

When the fighting ended, Roman dead covered the field of battle. Among them were "three of the tribunes who had been chiefly instrumental in urging the Consul to risk the engagement." Before the battle these jealous messmates of Scipio's had scoffed at his urgent recommendations for caution. Possibly among the dead tribunes was the one who had even angrily "threatened to throw away his sword if Scipio, instead of Manilius, were to command the expedition."

Scipio's final achievement in this campaign was to bring about the only act of chivalry recorded in the war. He sent a Carthaginian captive to Hasdrubal requesting suitable burial for the dead tribunes, who were easy to identify because they wore gold signet rings whereas the legionaries had iron rings. Hasdrubal buried them as Scipio desired.

While the surviving Romans retreated, Phameas attacked their flanks and rear. And as they drew near their camp outside Carthage, the city's defenders sallied forth to deal them still another blow.

The Roman system of command must bear part of the responsibility for the Roman failure. Manilius commanded the Roman army for one year because the citizens had elected him consul for those twelve months and political appeal rarely accompanied military ability. Manilius certainly showed very little. His reckless campaign is a perfect example, often met in Roman history, of a consul approaching the end of his term of office and taking foolish risks in the hope of winning a victory and a coveted Roman triumph.

But the Roman army had not suffered an irreparable defeat; it had escaped annihilation. Its morale, however, fell to a new low. And in Carthage, the morale of the people and of their defenders soared.

In this campaign, the consul's strategy of the indirect approach and his objective were entirely correct. When he made the mobile Carthaginian army in the field his objective instead of the fortified city which he had found impregnable, his strategy showed an improvement long overdue. Hasdrubal's army posed a threat which he could never ignore. It protected a rich and convenient granary for Carthage. Sound strategy required that this army be destroyed as a prelude to an attack or siege of the city.

But Manilius failed utterly as a tactician. In spite of Scipio's warnings he fell into a trap from which he could hardly have escaped without Scipio's intervention. Obviously he had no eye for terrain. Even in a most superficial reconnaissance, a good tactician would have seen how the little stream with its high banks would be an obstacle to movement and maneuver in battle. If he attacked as he did, the terrain would decrease his mobility almost to the vanishing point. Moreover, by the standards of his own times, he neglected security by engaging in battle without fortifying a camp. He showed little potential for leading an army to victory.

In reading Appian, it is difficult to avoid the suspicion that the historian has not resisted the temptation to emphasize the military ineptitude of the unfortunate Manilius in order to contrast Scipio's military virtues. As the story progresses, however, Manilius achieves nothing to retrieve his reputation.

The Roman Senate had the power to scrutinize the acts of

consuls commanding armies in the field. The series of defeats necessitated a senatorial investigation on the spot. So "the Senate sent commissioners to the army to obtain and communicate to it accurate particulars." For the first time we find an understatement in Appian. This senatorial committee on the conduct of the war would naturally search out and pinpoint the responsibility for the state of affairs in North Africa.

As usual, our source is silent on everything the committee learned, except, of course, what concerns Scipio. There is no intent here to deride Appian's admiration for Scipio, which was well deserved. Nevertheless, it is regrettable that in his enthusiasm Appian neglects other important information which would dispel some of the many uncertainties that beset the chronicle of the Third Punic War.

The committee heard testimony, and returned to Rome to report. What fascinating reading those findings and conclusions would be today! But Appian says that the committee heard unanimous praise of Scipio and his military skill. From Manilius to the newest recruit, the whole army agreed that the youthful Scipio had become the hero of officers and men.

"These things [about Scipio] greatly pleased the Senate," Appian wrote, "but on account of the many mishaps that had taken place they sent to Masinissa to secure his utmost aid against Carthage." It was an astonishing turnabout. In the beginning of the war, Rome had preferred to go it alone, snubbing Masinissa in the hope that history would record that Rome had defeated Carthage without outside aid. And Masinissa, while he did not go over to the Carthaginians, as they had hoped, had sat out the war. Now Rome had had to swallow her pride. The Senate sent envoys to Masinissa; but it was too late. The king was dead. He had fought a good fight for Rome and for his gods and his country. He did not live to see the ultimate purpose of his life achieved. He did not reach his goal of creating a vast kingdom under his rule extending from the Atlantic to Egypt. His work would result in Roman dominion of that area and would leave Numidia a client kingdom of Rome. He could not have guessed that Jugurtha, a grand-son of his, thirty-eight years later would lead the Numidians in a bitter war against Rome.

When he had felt death approaching, "he had asked Scipio on the ground of his friendship with him and with his grandfather, to come and consult with him concerning his children and the government." Scipio went, but he did not arrive in time. The succession to Masinissa's throne was complicated because the inheritance was to be divided among three legitimate sons. But Scipio, as shrewd a diplomat as solider, solved the dilemma to the satisfaction of all concerned. He divided the power and the glory and the wealth of Numidia equally.

To the [three] legitimate sons he gave in common the treasures and the revenues and the title of king. The other things he divided as he judged fitting, according to the disposition of each. To Micipsa, the oldest, a lover of peace, he assigned the city of Cirta and the royal palace there. Gulussa, a man of warlike parts and the next in age, he made arbiter of peace and war. Mastanabal, the youngest, who was a man of upright life, was appointed judge to decide causes between their subjects.

Among the heirs of Alexander the Great, such a settlement invited fraternal strife and bloodshed. But this did not happen in Numidia—a rare exception in ancient history—and Scipio's arbitration evidences once more the qualities of this extraordinary man, who when he was called on in 149 B.C. to settle Masinissa's estate, was only a thirty-six-year-old tribune. But his decisions influenced the outcome of the Third Punic War. He brought the Numidians back into active military participation as Rome's allies, adding the strength that Rome needed to weight the balance of power and precluding the possibility that Numidia might change sides.

Scipio lost no time in organizing Numidian aid. Masinissa's warrior son, Gulussa, took on the mission of pursuing Phameas, finding his base of operations and stopping his destructive raids.

If Rome had its Scipio, Carthage had its Phameas, who quite possibly was the mind and the soul of Hasdrubal's army.

But luck was with Scipio. One day he came face to face with Phameas across an impassable stream. Apparently Phameas wanted to say something to Scipio. When they were out of hearing of their companions, Scipio asked Phameas: "Why do you not look out for your own safety since you cannot do anything for your country's?"

Phameas undoubtedly had been one of the Carthaginian leaders condemned to death along with Hasdrubal in the effort to appease Rome and had not forgotten his government's contemptible act. Phameas replied to Scipio that he had damaged the Roman cause so much that he could not expect safety if he personally surrendered. Scipio promised him pardon and favor of the Romans if he gave himself up. After considerable cogitation, Phameas communicated to Scipio his decision to desert. The two met at the head of their cavalry detachments. Phameas moved forward between the lines and told his staff:

If there is any chance of rendering service to our country I am ready to stand by you for that purpose, but in the existing state of things, I am going to look out for my own safety. I have made terms for myself and for as many of you as I can persuade to join me. It is time for you too to consider what is for your advantage.

Some of the officers joined Phameas, taking with them about 2,200 men.

It is difficult to avoid the suspicion that Phameas's words, "the existing state of things," included his contempt for Hasdrubal. What the loss of Phameas meant to Carthage is emphasized by the testimony of both Livy and Appian. In the Summaries of the former's lost book, Livy calls Phameas "a brave man who was of extraordinary service to the Carthaginians," and Appian writes that when Scipio returned with Phameas, "the army went out to meet him and saluted him with cheers as in a triumph."

Phameas's defection even redeemed, Manilius thought, his first defeat at Nepheris, and the utter failure of a second expedition to that place which he had made a month later without daring to offer battle. He had feared disgrace on his return to Rome. But the defection of Phameas had provided him with a resounding victory, and he would finish his year as consul with something to his credit. It was time. The new consul, Calpurnius Piso, would arrive in a few months.

Manilius sent Scipio to Rome with his prize. The departure from Africa and the reception in Rome were notable events worthy of recording in Appian's brief account of the war. He reports:

> The army conducted Scipio to the ship with acclamations and prayed that he might return to Africa as consul, because they thought that he alone could take Carthage, for the opinion had sprung up among them, as by divine inspiration, that only Scipio would take Carthage, and many of them wrote to this effect to their relatives in Rome. The Senate praised Scipio and bestowed on Phameas a purple robe with gold clasps, a horse with gold trappings, a complete suit of armor, and 10,000 drachmas of silver money. They also gave him 100 minas of silver plate and a tent completely furnished, and told him that he might expect more if he would cooperate with them to the end of the war. He promised to do so and set sail for the Roman camp in Africa.

Phameas appears no more in the pages of history. But we may safely estimate that his loss to Carthage was equivalent to the addition of many legions to the Roman army.

Among the myriad admirers of Scipio in Rome was the aged Cato. When tidings of Scipio's good judgment and achievements reached Rome, Cato quoted from the Odyssey: "Only he has wits, but the rest are fluttering shadows." Shortly after that Cato breathed his last. Thus both Cato and Masinissa, the two chief executioners of Carthage, died in 149 B.C., a year of amazing triumphs for Carthage and of humiliating defeats for Rome.

XV

THE SECOND YEAR: 148 B.C.

Manilius, awaiting the arrival of his successor in the early months of 148 B.C., had good reason to wonder whether he was besieging Carthage or whether Carthage was besieging him. Since his second Nepheris campaign, with its comic march up hill and down again without a fight, he had not dared to move far beyond the confines of his two camps. Nearly all his supplies had to be brought from overseas. The defending army in Carthage and the army of Nepheris twenty miles away threatened his front and his rear. So Manilius sat still.

Calpurnius Piso, one of the new consuls, arrived at his headquarters in Utica about the end of March. The other consul stayed home, because serious dangers to Rome's security, including war in Macedonia, required his presence there. Scipio too remained in Rome, engaging in politics and enjoying the company of poets, philosophers, and historians. The second-in-command in the war against Carthage was a *legatus*, Lucius Mancinus, who was assigned to command the fleet. No records give the strength of the land and naval forces that Piso took over, or say how they were deployed, but presumably the two camps close to Carthage maintained the blockade and the situation remained unchanged from the previous year.

With the help of Lucius Mancinus, Piso planned a joint army-navy operation. The Romans knew that Carthaginian ships had run the blockade, and so far hunger had not caused much

139

suffering in the city. Since the direct approach of his predecessor had failed, Piso decided on an indirect approach, in which he would concentrate on destroying Carthage's food supply. His first objective was the Cape Bon peninsula, whence food and other necessities were sailed to Carthage across the Gulf of Tunis. To it the Roman fleet convoyed that part of the army assigned to this campaign.

The Cape Bon peninsula stretches about fifty miles into the Mediterranean. Although it includes some fairly high mountains, there has always been ample space in the fifteen to twenty-five miles breadth for many large estates as well as for small farms. There are no good harbors on the peninsula, but beaches, especially around the prospective point of attack, Clupea, provided berths for warships.

This peninsula, which gained prominence once more in World War II, when the Allies regarded it as the potential site of a last-ditch stand by the Germans in Africa, had played an important role in earlier invasions of North Africa. Agathocles, the king of Syracuse, and Regulus, the Roman consul in the First Punic War, had landed there to begin their invasions. The small city known to the Greeks as Aspis and to the Romans as Clupea was well named. Its site closely resembles a round shield of bull's hide, overlaid with a boss in the middle (Greek *aspis*, Latin *clipeus*), lying flat on the ground. Today, the Tunisian town of Kélibia, named after Clupea, is a few miles from the coast, and a medieval fortress occupies the summit of the hill where the ancient Clupea stood behind ramparts overlooking the Mediterranean. The summit of this hill is about 250 feet above sea level. Polybius reports that in the First Punic War the Romans under Regulus, "landing there and beaching their ships, which they surrounded with a trench and palisade, . . . set themselves to lay siege to the town."

In 148 B.C. Piso evidently followed this same plan. But Clupea repulsed the attack and Piso eventually gave up the siege, destroying instead a neighboring town. Undoubtedly he repeated the devastation of earlier invasions, when first the Greeks and then the Romans looted and razed villas and seized cattle and thousands of slaves. This unsuccessful campaign on Cape Bon, although temporarily disrupting to economic resources, must have taken most of April and May in 148 B.C. The results were by no means commensurate with the time and the cost of the campaign.

Piso then transferred his army by sea to his next objective, the city of Hippagreta, today Bizerte. This was an important Carthaginian city which had remained loyal to the metropolis, and which was ideally located, as the map shows, for interfering with the overseas supply line of the Roman army. The Bizertan builders and owners of the privateers engaged in this business were growing wealthy, and the Romans were growing hungry. Bizerte must be blotted out. Unfortunately for Piso, the city was strongly fortified and bravely defended. Appian reports that:

After besieging Bizerte the whole summer he accomplished nothing. Twice the inhabitants made sallies with the aid of the Carthaginians, and burned the Roman battering rams, protective sheds, and catapults. The consul, being foiled, returned to Utica and went into winter quarters.

Carthage's successes were earning dividends. A Numidian chief named Bithya deserted to Carthage with a cavalry force of eight hundred. Two of Masinissa's sons, Micipsa and Mastanabal, were not keeping their promises to aid Rome with money and weapons, perhaps in the belief that their cousin, Hasdrubal Numidianus, might bring about a union of Carthage and Numidia against Rome.

The Carthaginians moved freely over all their territory, fortifying towns and addressing the people in speeches disparaging the Romans. "In proof of the Romans' cowardice they pointed out the two victories at Nepheris and the more recent one at

Hippagreta [Bizerte], and to Carthage itself, which the enemy had not been able to take although it was unarmed and poorly defended."

Their two years of successful resistance made possible a stronger foreign policy. They asked Micipsa and Mastanabal for Numidian aid. They sent envoys to the free Moors to ask support and tried to persuade them that if Carthage were defeated, they would be the next victims of Rome's imperialism. Ambassadors traveled to Andriscus, who claimed to be a son of King Perseus, and who in 148 was pretender to the throne of Macedonia and at war with Rome, urging him to fight with all his might, and promising him money and ships. "Being now armed, their designs grew unbounded, and they gained in confidence, courage, and resources from day to day." But later in 148 Rome sent Quintus Caesilius Metellus across the Adriatic with a large army and, before that year ended, a military victory finished Andriscus's career and Carthage's hope of a Macedonian alliance.

If Carthage had had a Hamilcar or a Hannibal in 148 B.C., she might have won at least a favorable peace. But Carthage had Hasdrubal. At this moment he and his countrymen were

in high spirits. Aspiring to the command in the city, which was held by another Hasdrubal, a nephew of Gulussa, he accused this Hasdrubal [Numidianus] of an intention to betray Carthage to Gulussa. This accusation being brought forward in the assembly, and the accused being at a loss to answer the unexpected charge, they fell upon him and beat him to death with the benches.

The murder of the general who had defended Carthage so skillfully for more than a year is inexplicable in Western terms. Remembering Phameas, they were easily swayed by Hasdrubal. So little is known of the life of Hasdrubal Numidianus that we can only judge him by the fruits of his labors. His monument is the epic defense of Carthage, monument more enduring than bronze.

In other crises, the gods had been kind to Carthage. Xanthippus, the Spartan soldier of fortune, had defeated Regulus in the First Punic War, and saved the city. Hamilcar Barca had rescued it from the rebellious mercenaries. Hannibal had proved what a Carthaginian general could achieve. But with the death of Hasdrubal Numidianus, Carthage had to depend on the other Hasdrubal. He was a weak reed upon which to lean.

After Oroscopa, he had offered to surrender though he had hardly been beaten. His victory over Manilius was a tactical masterpiece, it is true, but Phameas may have had much to do with it.

Polybius, who knew him personally, considered him a *Miles Gloriosus* of Roman comedy. He looked and acted like an early Falstaff. The Latin phrase fits him perfectly: *Vox et praeterea nihil*—a voice and nothing else, for his brave words bore no resemblance to his cowardly actions. Subsequent events confirm Polybius's characterization.

If Livy had called Hasdrubal "an empty-headed braggart" the estimate might be questioned, for Livy rarely viewed Rome's enemies impartially, but Polybius was objective, even where his beloved Rome and his native Greece were concerned. Hasdrubal undoubtedly earned the contempt Polybius felt for him. Physical courage he may have had, but too little is known about him to credit him with it. Moral courage, however, he did not have: his own acts attest to that, for at the most important moments of his life he displayed timidity. As Polybius implies, weakness of character was his greatest deficiency for command. Carthage, like Athens, elected its generals, but there is no evidence that Carthage, like Athens, required candidates for military leadership to submit to an examination of character, which was, in fact, the only

143

test they had to pass. Hasdrubal never would have passed it, yet he was the general on whom Carthage's survival now depended.

In 149 and 148 Rome was plagued even more than Carthage by inept generals. The abortive military efforts which had nearly lost the war had sharpened internal dissension. But Rome's political system made a change in government and military command relatively easy. The two consuls with supreme civil and military authority were elected each year, and the elections were close at hand. The Roman people determined to elect a consul with proven military skill.

Who else was there but Scipio? All Rome knew of his exploits. But he was only thirty-seven years old, and a consul had to be at least forty-three. But the people elected him anyway, and defied objections that they had acted illegally. So the law was suspended for one year. In addition, the people, quite contrary to custom, chose Scipio to command in Africa.

He was authorized to obtain reinforcements through conscription to make good all losses suffered in 148. He was granted authority to enlist volunteers among Rome's allies "and in consequence he did obtain some assistance from them." He had also a considerable piece of good fortune: Rome had defeated Macedonia in 148, and no longer had to fear a formal alliance of Macedonia and Carthage. The severe drain on her resources caused by the need to fight a two-front war in 148 was now ended. In that year there may have been a lull in the war with the Spanish tribes, but in 147 that guerrilla war will grow more violent and more difficult to win.

XVI

SCIPIO TAKES COMMAND

The Ides of March of 147 B.C. had come and gone. By the end of the month weather was suitable for navigation in the Mediterranean. With the enthusiastic support of the Senate and the people, Scipio embarked for North Africa, where Piso, far from Carthage, was attempting to capture as many cities and towns as possible before Scipio replaced him. His soldiers were looting the areas they overran, far more intent on booty than military victory. Mancinus and his fleet were at his base in Utica, a four- or five-hour sail from the Carthaginian harbors; apparently he too saw one last chance for glory, and with more fortitude than foresight, he planned a surprise naval raid on Carthage which might even win the war before Scipio arrived. His plan of action was the scheme of a bold and daring sailor.

On his journeys from his base in Utica to Carthage, Mancinus had frequently rounded an imposing headland where now the white walls of the Arab village of Sidi-bou-Said crown the summit, and where then the ramparts of Carthage topped the steep, red cliff more than 400 feet high. Nature had defended no other sector of the city walls as strongly as here, and Mancinus surmised correctly that it would have few defenders. No one could reasonably anticipate an assault up this abrupt cliff, so an attack would find the enemy asleep and unprepared. The position was far from the center of the Carthaginian mobile defense reserves, and aid would be several hours away.

Ladders for scaling the city wall had to be carried by hand up the long, nearly vertical slope, but the ladders also helped the climb up the cliff. Some of the five hundred Romans in the raiding party had even reached the top of the wall, when the few Carthaginian defenders on duty rushed out of a gate to counter-attack. The Romans, in superior numbers, drove the Carthaginians back and pursued them through the gate into the city. "They raised a shout of victory and Mancinus, transported with joy [for he was rash and light-minded by nature] and the whole crowd with him, rushed from the ships, unarmed or half-armed, to aid their companions." By this time the sun was setting.

Now it was Mancinus who had become the besieged, for the Carthaginians had rallied and backed him up against the city ramparts. The five hundred armed men of the raiding party formed a semicircular line of defense behind which Mancinus and the three thousand unarmed men from the fleet helplessly awaited the dawn. Mancinus sent a ship to Utica for help and food and he called on the distant Piso to rush soldiers. He knew that by morning Carthaginian reserves would arrive in superior numbers. Surrender or death by being dashed to pieces over the brink of the precipice were the alternatives.

Scipio had reached Utica that evening, and about midnight learned of the predicament of Mancinus and his men. The crews of his convoy were resting after their journey from Lilybaeum, the Roman base in Sicily, where Scipio had paused. In those times the hundred miles of sailing from Sicily to Utica took a convoy about two days and nights, during which the men in their crowded transports had little sleep.

But Scipio was not a man to delay a rescue operation. Appian writes that "he ordered the trumpets to sound for battle im-mediately, and the heralds to call to the sea-shore those who had come with him from Italy, and also the young men of Utica, and he directed the older men to bring provisions to the gal-leys." He also sent mounted messengers to Piso to expedite his return from his march up-country.

Then Scipio, a master of psychological warfare, released some Carthaginian prisoners to report his arrival to their countrymen, knowing how demoralizing the news would be. While it was still night he put to sea. He crowded his ships with soldiers, ordering them to stand on the decks to make a show of strength when they came in sight of the wall behind which Mancinus was surrounded.

At dawn Carthaginian reinforcements arrived and started their attack, which would have succeeded in destroying or capturing every member of this Roman raiding party, had not "Scipio's fleet come in sight amidst terrible clouds of spray, with soldiers crowding the decks everywhere." The morale of the hard-pressed Romans rose; the spirit of the Carthaginians faltered. The Carthaginians drew back. Mancinus and his men escaped—the men to fight another day, Mancinus to return home ingloriously. Scipio had done it again.

A sketch of Scipio in Dio's *Roman History* provides an explanation of how he was able to succeed, again and again.

This man [Scipio Africanus] excelled in planning out at leisure the requisite course, but excelled also in discovering the immediate need on the spur of the moment, and was able to employ either method on the proper occasion. The duties that lay before him he examined coldly, but performed them as if with timidity. Hence, by his fearless and deliberate examination of matters he understood exactly the proper thing to do, and would accomplish it safely as a result of the thought he gave to the element of uncertainty. Accordingly, if he was ever brought face to face with some crisis that admitted of no deliberation, such as is wont to happen in the contradictions of warfare and the turns of fortune, not even then did he miss the proper course. For, thanks to his habit of never trusting recklessly to luck for anything, he was not unprepared for the assault of a sudden emergency, but through his incessant activity was able to meet even the unexpected as if he had long foreseen it. As a result he showed himself exceedingly bold in matters where he felt he was right, and likewise exceedingly venturesome where he felt bold; for in physique he was as powerful as the best of the soldiers. This led to one of his most remarkable characteristics: he would devise the most advantageous plans as if he were going to direct others, and at the time of action would execute them as if they had been ordered by others. Besides not swerving from the ordinary paths of rectitude, he kept faith scrupulously not only with the citizens and his associates, but even with foreigners and the bitterest enemies; and this brought many individuals as well as many cities to his side. He never acted or even spoke without due consideration, nor through anger or fear, but through the certainty of his calculations was ready for all occasions; he took sufficiently into account the instability of human plans, and yet regarded nothing as impossible, but deliberated every matter beforehand in the light of its real nature. Thus he perceived very easily the right course to follow even before there was any necessity, and pursued it with firmness. Because of this, as well as because of his moderation and amiability, he alone of men, or at least more than others, escaped the envy of his peers, as well as of everyone else. For he chose to make himself the equal of his inferiors, not better than his equals, and inferior to greater men, and so passed beyond the reach of jealousy, which is the one thing that injures the noblest men.

In a few words, Plutarch, in his life of Tiberius Gracchus, summarizes Scipio's influence on his army: he had "a noble spirit —which was so fit to inspire strong feelings of emulation in virtue and desire to prove merit in action."

The Romans had a proverb that a general has the army he deserves. With Scipio at its head, the Roman army had an inestimable advantage over the Carthaginian army led by Hasdrubal.

Scipio started to build a camp for his army on the isthmus leading to the triple-defense line. To his amazement the enemy advanced about a thousand yards from that line and fortified a camp between Scipio and the city. Later Scipio learned that Hasdrubal and his new cavalry commander, Bithya, had joined the garrison of the advanced fort with six thousand infantry and a thousand cavalry. What could Hasdrubal expect to accomplish from this position? It was far beyond artillery support by catapults on the triple defense line. There were no ravines, swamps, streams, or other natural obstacles to help protect it from Roman assault. An advance line of a number of mutually supporting field fortifications might have delayed a Roman advance, but a single unsupported fort or redoubt that could be surrounded and starved out was the height of folly. Its only effect was to withhold probably ten thousand men from their proper duty as a strategic reserve in the city. At best, Hasdrubal's total forces were exceedingly small to man the city's twenty-mile defense line. Clearly Hasdrubal had learned nothing from the loss of his army by Masinissa's siege in 150 B.C.

Scipio could not begin any assault for some time. The army that Piso turned over to him was an armed mob, whose sole objective was booty: the winning of a war never entered its mind. Hundreds of camp followers, getting rich on plunder, created chaos. Scipio called his men together and from a high platform addressed them:

Soldiers, when I served with you under the command of Manilius, I gave you an example of obedience, as you can testify. I ask the same from you, now that I am in command; for while I have power to punish the disobedient with the utmost severity, I think it best to give you warning beforehand. You know what you have been doing. Therefore why should I tell you what I am ashamed to speak of? You are more like robbers than soldiers. You are runaways instead of guardians of the camp. Avarice has made you more like a set of holiday-makers than a besieging army. You are in quest of luxuries in the midst of war and before the victory is won. For this reason the enemy, from the hopeless weakness in which I left him, has risen to such strength, and your labor has been made harder by your laziness. If I considered you to blame for this I should punish you at once, but since I ascribe it to another, I shall overlook the past. I have come here not to rob, but to conquer, not to make money before victory, but to overcome the enemy first.

He ordered the camp followers to go at once. He promised spoils and luxury after Carthage had been taken but severe penalties for disobedience until the victory had been won.

Rehabilitation of his army required at least three or four weeks. When at last Scipio felt he had a reliable force, he put his plan of direct attack into operation. The assault would be made at night. Tactically, it was a vast improvement over the assaults of 149 b.c., and if it succeeded it would end the war. It was a test of the defenses and the defenders which Scipio could not avoid making if he was to win the quick victory that Rome demanded.

Scipio planned a combined frontal and flank attack with the help of some deserters to guide him when he penetrated the defenses. Piso, who apparently had been retained on duty by order of the Roman Senate, was to by-pass Hasdrubal's fort, and feint against the triple defense line. Scipio, farther north, would outflank the northern junction of the triple-defense line and the single wall, to make the main assault against that more vulnerable sector. His men, equipped with axes, scaling ladders, and crowbars, covered the two and a half miles from his camp to the point of attack in silence.

How much of his army of more than eighty thousand men engaged in the assault we do not know, but a considerable force must have been left behind to watch Hasdrubal. When the Carthaginians on the walls became aware of the advance they gave the alarm. The Romans answered with shouts from both front and flank attacks. The Carthaginians were badly frightened by the assault they could hear but not see; however, Scipio found the attack on the single wall as vain as had his predecessors. But he was lucky as well as brave; he had noticed a privately owned tower, now deserted, only a few feet outside the city walls and of the same height as the wall. He ordered a small detachment to enter the tower and to run to the roof. From there they killed the defenders on the city wall opposite with their javelins. They then bridged the gap with planks, descended into the town, and opened a gate, letting in Scipio with four thousand men. Appian does not mention Piso's activities which were unquestionably only a feint intended to disperse the defenders of the city and to conceal the real point of attack. But now a large part of the Roman army must have entered the city.

The terrain then became a potent ally of the Carthaginians. The Romans had penetrated Megara, the suburb where olive groves and orchards separated by hedges of brambles and thorns and by deep irrigation ditches made maneuver at night hazardous. Prudently, Scipio withdrew.

No Roman army had been trained for this kind of warfare. A battle should be fought between two lines of men facing each other on level and open ground. How could a Roman general control an engagement at night where the nature of the ground divided the army into scores, possibly hundreds, of little groups of which he could see only a few? The next day, Scipio destroyed Hasdrubal's redoubt which, as was to be anticipated, was no obstacle to the Roman night attack.

The accounts of this night attack in Appian and in Zonaras are obscure and confused. Nevertheless it is certain that when Hasdrubal heard the tumult of the attack, he and his troops abandoned his advanced redoubt and entered the city, halting only when he reached the citadel on the Byrsa, where other panicky Carthaginians had taken refuge. The next morning, when they discovered that Scipio had withdrawn, they were as angry at themselves as they were at the enemy.

Hasdrubal vented his wrath on Roman prisoners. He brought them upon the city walls where, Polybius says, he treated them "in such an inhuman manner" that it violated the laws of men. Appian describes the atrocities thus: Hasdrubal "in full sight of their comrades—tore out their eyes, tongues, tendons, or private parts with iron hooks; of some he lacerated the soles of the feet, of others he cut off the fingers, and some he flayed alive, hurling them all, still living, from the top of the walls."

Hasdrubal committed these crimes so that the Roman army as well as the Carthaginians could see them. The effect on the Roman army can easily be imagined. Appian says "he intended to make reconciliation between the Carthaginians and Romans impossible, and sought to fire them [the Carthaginians] with the conviction that their only safety was in fighting: but the result was contrary to his intentions."

In Carthage Hasdrubal's experiment in psychological warfare failed utterly. The Carthaginians were horrified. Conscience-stricken, they became timid instead of courageous. They feared Roman vengeance. Some courageous senators denounced Hasdrubal's savagery. Hasdrubal arrested and executed them. "Making himself feared in every way, he came to be more like a tyrant than a general, for he considered himself secure only if he were an object of terror to [his countrymen] and for this reason difficult to attack."

Nevertheless, the Carthaginian Senate "denounced Hasdrubal for committing these savage and outrageous cruelties in the midst of such great domestic calamities," which prompts the conclusion that the civil authorities continued to control Carthage.

Scipio's first attack had failed, but neither Hasdrubal and his army nor the city's defenses had caused his defeat. The terrain had beaten him. He had learned his lesson. He made no further assault for the time being and turned to his engineers. Fortunately for him, the Roman soldier was trained to use the spade as well as the sword.

XVII

ROME IN THE ASCENDANT

Polybius had tutored Scipio in the lessons to be learned from Alexander the Great's campaigns. The siege of Tyre had cost Alexander seven months of toil. But it had brought victory. Carthage posed problems as difficult as those at Tyre. Nevertheless Scipio made his decision.

After more than two years of war, foodstuffs and other supplies still entered the city of Carthage through two open doors. The Romans had done their best to close the doors, but neither Scipio's first camp nor the other legionary camps, designed on the standard model, covered more than a fraction of the width of the isthmus where the city's triple-defense line lay. Such camps could not prevent pack animals in small groups from carrying supplies into the city by night. Similarly, with favorable winds at night, blockade-runners easily voyaged from Cape Bon to the harbor mouth. Carthage hungered but did not starve. Scipio planned to shut both doors so tight that famine would bring Carthage to her knees.

Most reluctantly, Scipio had concluded that Carthage could not be taken by storm. The Romans in the night attack must have suffered far more than the records reveal; otherwise he would not have abandoned the direct approach for the slow and tedious task of reducing Carthage by starvation. Scipio's astounding engineering works were to be immensely costly to Rome in money and time but the work advanced with the inevitability of a glacier inching to the end of its course.

His first step was to begin constructing a massive fortification stretching for more than two miles across the isthmus. The fortification, designed to become the main camp for the Roman army, began with a straight, single trench running from the Lake of Tunis to the lagoon. It had to be dug two to three hundred yards from the Carthaginian fortifications which it paralleled to be beyond effective range of the catapults on the triple-defense line.

Scipio worked on this trench night and day, under constant interference from hostile sorties. While part of his army dug, the other legionaries slept, stood watch, or waited under arms to repel assaults from the city. When the trench was finished, Scipio dug a second parallel to the first. He then connected the ends of each long trench with two short trenches parallel to the shores of the lakes.

Each trench consisted of a parapet in front of which was a deep ditch with sharpened stakes in its bottom. Palisades surmounted the parapets on all sides of the fortification except on the front facing the city, which needed special strength. Along the entire length of this sector, Scipio built a wall twelve feet high and six feet wide, with towers at frequent intervals. In the center of that line stood a tower so high that from the top his sentinels could see into the city. This tower had a stone base topped by a four-story wooden structure. And thus Scipio closed the back door of the city: his fortification sealed off Carthage from approach by land. But supplies carried by blockade-runners still could reach the city, because the front door—the harbor entrance—remained open; the oar-propelled warships of the Roman fleet maintained an ineffective blockade.

In the meantime refugees from the surrounding country had swelled Carthage's population, so there were many useless mouths to feed on the supplies that the blockade-runners and an oc-

casional merchantman brought. Hasdrubal saw to it that his thirty
thousand soldiers were well fed, at the expense of civilians.
Furthermore Scipio's fort barred escape from the city, and the
civilians began to suffer the effects of hunger. Bithya, who with
his thousand cavalrymen had fled from the advanced redoubt into
the city the night Scipio attacked, had escaped before Scipio's
fort was completed. His base was in the old camp near Nepheris,
but he could hardly challenge Scipio's fort.

Scipio knew he had to close the entrance to the harbor. He
remembered how Alexander the Great had joined Tyre to the
mainland with a causeway to effect capture of the city. Alexander
had spent seven months at the siege, but the distance from Tyre
to the mainland was nearly eight hundred yards, part of it through
deep water. Scipio projected an embankment only a little more
than five hundred yards long, through water less deep. He had all
the men he needed to bring up the rocks and earth for the foundation. Moreover, although the Carthaginians could see the work
from their walls, for a long time they could do little to hinder
its progress. Scipio would not have to keep thousands of armed
men ready to repel sorties.

It was now the beginning of June. Weather would not be an
obstacle. Work could continue night and day. And after the three
months that Scipio estimated this prodigious effort would require,
Carthage, cut off from all food supplies except for whatever
blockade-runners could land on the exterior quay called the
Choma, would inevitably surrender.

Appian reports that the mole was started from the tongue of
land, the Taenia, lying between the Lake of Tunis and the sea.
He does not mention the location of the other end, which must
have been the massive stone wharf called the Choma. Appian
notes that the mole was "twenty-four feet wide at the top and
four times as wide at the bottom." The Carthaginians derided
the project, calculating that it might take a year or more to complete, and perhaps might never be finished. As the work pro-

gressed, the Carthaginians probably imitated their kinsmen in Tyre who taunted Alexander's soldiers because these men "famous in arms were carrying loads on their backs like pack mules." Zonaras reports that the Carthaginians naturally interfered with the work and that many skirmishes occurred. But Scipio's men had reason to work hard and fast—and fight when necessary. They never forgot the booty that would reward them when they took Carthage.

Before the mole was completed, the Carthaginians sprang a surprise of a kind rarely encountered in the annals of warfare, and all the more remarkable because it required resourcefulness and initiative by a hungry and desperate people. When the Carthaginians saw that the end of the mole approached the wharf and that already no ships could enter their harbor, they started to build a fleet. Behind the high wall which surrounded their naval base and the commercial harbor with its docks and shipyards, they constructed fifty triremes and many smaller ships in utter secrecy. Scipio heard from prisoners that all day and all night there was noise in the harbor areas. What caused it, the prisoners did not know. Scipio wondered, but was not alarmed. He could hardly have imagined that the enemy was building a fleet to challenge Roman sea power. He had seen to it that no ships could reach or leave Carthage's harbor. There was the high wall on the city's sea front. There was no entrance other than the one he was closing.

But the Carthaginians had a plan. While the ships were building, they began to dig a channel from the circular naval harbor through the few yards of land between the harbor's edge and the city wall. At the last minute they would tear down a section of the wall and then the fleet, built of timber which had been stored for the purpose or taken from demolished buildings, would sail to do battle.

Thousands of artisans worked day and night for several months to build the fleet. Women and children strained their backs to help dig a channel out of the naval base.

D-day arrived. Planning and the work was done. "Finally, everything being finished, the Carthaginians opened the new entrance about dawn, and passed out with fifty triremes, besides pinnaces, brigantines, and smaller craft equipped in a way to cause terror." The Roman fleet, now that the mole closed the harbor mouth, had abandoned its blockade. As the Carthaginians could see from the city walls, the Roman ships were beached, awaiting the end of the war. Sailors and rowers had been called to other duties, probably to help complete the mole.

There was hope in Carthage that morning. The new harbor entrance could never be blocked by siege works: the water was too deep, and the winds frequently too high for such construction. Food would soon reach Carthage. The army at Nepheris had food and it had the ships to carry it. As Appian puts it: "The Romans were so astounded by the sudden appearance of this new entrance [to the harbor] and the fleet issuing from it, that if the Carthaginians had at once fallen upon their ships . . . they might have possessed themselves of the whole fleet."

Victory might have come all the easier because, as Appian explains, the Romans had neglected their own fleet in recent months. "But . . . all they [the Carthaginians] did now was to sail out and make a show, and, after flouting the enemy in a pompous way, to return inside the harbor."

Carthage (or was it Hasdrubal?) missed a rare chance. A naval triumph that day might not have given Carthage total victory, but it might have gained a reasonable peace—or attracted new allies.

Appian goes on:

Three days later they [the Carthaginians] set out for a naval engagement, and the Romans advanced to meet them with their ships and everything else in good order. Loud were the cheers on both sides as they came together; and rowers, helmsmen, and marines exerted themselves to the utmost, this being the last hope of safety for the Carthaginians and of complete victory for the Romans. The fight raged till midday. During the battle the small boats of the Carthaginians stove holes in the sterns of the taller Roman ships. They broke off their oars and rudders and damaged them considerably in various other ways, advancing and retreating handily. But when toward evening, the battle was still undecided, the Carthaginians thought best to withdraw, not that they were defeated, but in order to renew the engagement the next day.

When the fifty triremes and seventy smaller craft had rowed out of the naval base, the admiral from his tower command post had kept strict order at the channel. There was no disorder, no confusion, as the admiral signaled each ship in turn to move out. After the day's battle, control from the outside was difficult. The many small boats, which reached the mouth of the channel first, tangled hopelessly in the narrow passage and blocked the triremes. The best they could do was to tie up perpendicular to the merchant-ship wharf, the Choma. The triremes, side by side, bows facing outward, were easy targets for ramming tactics, and the Roman fleet drove at top speed against the Carthaginians. Carthage's fleet suffered considerable damage but the Romans did not escape unscathed. Carthage had built a parapet around the wharf, which was just outside the city walls. Now the catapults on it hurled sixty-pound stone projectiles and heavy arrows at the Roman warships. Soldiers lining the parapet and marines from the decks found the Roman crews and ships inviting targets for arrows and javelins. When the Romans, after delivering their blows, had to turn to move out to sea, the slow maneuver enabled the Carthaginians to inflict as much damage as they had suffered.

But the captains of five Greek warships with the Roman fleet had an idea. These Greeks handled ships better than did the Romans. To avoid the vulnerability of a 180-degree turn, the

Greeks dropped anchors with long ropes off the stern. They rowed at top speed to ram the Carthaginians. Then, having delivered the blow, they warped themselves stern foremost by the anchor ropes to ready themselves for the next charge. The Romans quickly followed their example. Now they damaged the Carthaginians with little loss to themselves. "Night put an end to the battle, after which the Carthaginian ships withdrew to the city, as many of them as were still left."

Thus vanished the last chance of the Carthaginians for victory at sea. Their effort deserved a better fate. Few if any military surprises had been better conceived, better planned, better carried out than this secret construction of a new fleet. But the use of this surprise was fantastically inept.

They had repeated the fiasco of 203 B.C., when a task force of the Carthaginian navy surprised Scipio Africanus the Elder and his fleet at Utica, but missed the opportunity to destroy the enemy fleet (see chap. VI). On both occasions the sortie of a Carthaginian fleet was a dramatic achievement that stunned the Romans. The Carthaginians had accomplished not only the unexpected; they had done the apparently impossible. Their measures to ensure secrecy of preparation were miraculously successful. But they failed utterly to profit from the surprise they obtained at the cost of so much labor.

Carthaginian sea power, reborn to survive only four days, had fought its last fight. The battered remnant of the fleet retired into the naval base behind the ramparts and no Carthaginian warship ever again sailed the Mediterranean. But the Carthaginians still had no thought of surrender.

By this time—about the end of August—the Roman engineers had almost completed the mole. Probably only a few yards of shallow water separated the end of the mole from the fortified Choma. Carthage's defenders had erected on this quay towers facing the end of the mole, when this harbor-blocking causeway was nearly completed.

At dawn on the day after the Carthaginian fleet had given up the struggle, Scipio began his assault on the Choma with fire from his catapults, supplemented by battering rams: the siege engines were mounted on the end of the causeway and on ships. No legionaries attempted to land on the Choma that day, which suggests that the missiles and rams succeeded in destroying only small sections of the parapet. When evening came, Scipio had failed to seize the Choma—which he had to reach to enable his engineers to complete the causeway and to occupy the wharf where a daring blockade-runner could still land supplies for the hungry city.

That night the Carthaginians replied with a desperately courageous and extremely effective counterattack against the enemy battering rams, catapults, and protective sheds.

No land approach was possible and the water was too shallow for boats, so the Romans anticipated no attack. Men on guard after the day-long struggle were presumably enjoying a well-earned rest. Suddenly the quiet of the night was shattered. Naked Carthaginians waded and swam stealthily, carrying torches which they lit only when they reached the rams and the catapults. They set fire to the wooden contraptions, creating panic among the Romans, who fled in disorder.

Panic and confusion [says Appian] spread through the whole camp and such fear as they had never before known, caused by the frenzy of these naked enemies. Scipio, fearing the consequences, ran out with a squadron of horse and commanded his men to kill those of his own troops who would not stop running away. Some of them he killed himself. The rest were brought forcibly into camp where they passed the night under arms, fearing the desperation of the enemy. The latter, after burning the Roman siege weapons, swam back home.

The next morning the Carthaginians, no longer hampered by missiles or rams, repaired the battered wall on the Choma, increased the wall's height and built more towers. The Choma had now become a fort outside the city walls.

But Scipio was no Censorinus; he did not give up. He extended the mole to the Choma, and he must have widened its end for his contemplated assault. His engineers constructed new rams and protective sheds. They built mounds as high as the Carthaginian towers—a traditional tactic in sieges of antiquity—from which to throw fire bombs at the enemy towers to ignite and destroy them. In the long run, Roman superiority in men and material overwhelmed the Carthaginians. The besieging army finally seized and in turn fortified the Choma, on which Scipio built a solid brick wall, parallel and within a javelin cast of the Carthaginian ramparts, which it equaled in height. Four thousand Romans garrisoned this Choma fort, and then overwhelming fire power with missiles and javelins kept the enemy off his parallel wall.

"And now the summer came to an end," says Appian opening his next paragraph with this sentence: "At the beginning of winter, Scipio resolved to destroy the Carthaginian armed forces in the country, and the allies from whom supplies were sent to them." Apparently the supplies entered through the hole in the sea wall used by the fleet in the surprise attack at the end of August; apparently the Roman fleet could not maintain an effective blockade.

Since starvation of the inhabitants and garrison of Carthage was the weapon on which Scipio relied to bring about surrender, his objective must now become the source of supplies, rather belatedly, it would seem. These were the areas of the Medjerda River valley and the Cape Bon peninsula and the fertile regions south of it in Africa.

The supplies were gathered by the Carthaginian army operating from Nepheris and from the strongly fortified camp a few miles from Nepheris, and shipped across the Gulf of Tunis. The small, fragile warships of the Punic War, unable to stay long at sea without intolerable discomfort to the crews, could not keep them out.

Scipio's tactical plan was to put into practice the recommendation he had made to Manilius two years earlier for his maneuver on this same battlefield, and to avoid Manilius's errors. The Carthaginian commander of Nepheris and the fortified camp was Diogenes, doubtless a Greek *condottiere*, who had succeeded Hasdrubal in command of this area.

Appian, unfortunately not at his best as a military historian, preserves only a few facts of this campaign and siege. Most of the details must be deduced from actual study of the ground. The site of Nepheris is known; the position of the Carthaginian camp is fixed by events described in the battle of 149; the location of Scipio's camp is suggested by his recommendations to Manilius in the first battle near Nepheris, and confirmed by Appian's statement that it was only a quarter of a mile from the Carthaginian camp.

Scipio divided his army into two columns for the move to Nepheris. His second in command, Gaius Laelius, marched via Tunis around the lake, while Scipio crossed the Lake of Tunis with the other legions, no doubt transporting by water his heavy siege equipment. From Scipio's landing place to these objectives was not many miles, but Nepheris was at an elevation of eight hundred feet and the enemy camp 460 feet above sea level. Assuming this campaign started about October 1, 147 B.C., preparations for the siege of both the camp and Nepheris would hardly have been completed before October 15.

A Numidian army under Gulussa joined the Romans at the beginning of the campaign. How many men were involved on either side is unrecorded. Appian says that after the battle for the camp, seventy thousand dead, including noncombatants, were counted, but the figure seems too high.

As the Romans and Numidians fortified their own camp and surrounded Diogenes and his men to cut off their supplies, the

Carthaginians probably made frequent sorties. Scipio maintained close personal supervision of his forces at Nepheris and Carthage, frequently visiting both fronts. Since his siege works surrounding the camp and Nepheris would ultimately cause their surrender through starvation, he may well have avoided an early assault. Moreover he had accomplished his primary mission of halting the shipment of supplies to the city.

Scipio had left Gulussa in charge of the attack on the camp. While the Numidian harassed the enemy by frequent assaults—which were not pressed home—Roman engineers attacked the camp's ramparts. The camp had become a powerful field fortification, with strong curtain walls between towers. By the end of November, the siege work had demolished two of the curtain walls.

Scipio was now ready to make a final assault on the Carthaginian camp. He organized and trained two groups of men selected for bravery. The larger detachment, three thousand strong, would make the main attack on a 400-foot front of the enemy camp after the wall was demolished.

To hide the preparations was impossible. Diogenes strengthened his front; he probably thought this was to be the only attack, although feints at other points would be good tactics that Scipio would hardly neglect.

The assault, when it came, must have been preceded by a bombardment from the Roman catapults. Then three thousand men in successive lines, closely following each other, charged, every man yelling at the top of his voice. Appian reports that the attack was made "in detachments one after the other, so that even if those in front were repulsed they could not retreat on account of the weight of those coming behind." From Diogenes down, everyone in the Carthaginian camp concentrated on repelling this attack. This was the moment Scipio awaited. He had concealed the thousand men of the other detachment in the wood behind the enemy camp. When the uproar of the battle in front reached them, they mounted the rear rampart, scaled the wall, and tore down the palisade in accordance with their orders. As they moved through the camp, the Carthaginians, believing the Romans to be there in larger numbers than they were, ran for their lives. The panic communicated itself to the surrounded soldiers in the camp. Every man, each for himself, sought safety in flight. Gulussa pursued them with his Numidian cavalry and trampled them with his elephants.

Gradually the noise of battle died down in the triangular valley. The high, forest-covered mountains looked down on tens of thousands of dead. But Nepheris still stood in solitary and forbidding strength on its pinnacle.

Twenty-two days later, in the wintry weather of December, Scipio took Nepheris too.

What happened to Carthage after the fall of Nepheris confirms Hannibal's statement, profoundly true both for hot and cold wars: "If you gain a victory even those who hate you will hold to you; if you are defeated even your friends will leave you."

The towns and villages, still free, which had supported Carthage, surrendered or fell after brief resistance. All that remained of the Carthaginian empire was Carthage itself.

At this stage of the siege, not even Hannibal himself could have saved Carthage. But in early May, 147, a Hannibal, as sagacious in negotiation as he was brilliant in military strategy, might have negotiated a peace to end the war so ruinous to both Carthage and Rome. On December 31, the sands had run out. It was too late. But Carthage still possessed the will to fight.

XVIII

THE FINAL AGONY

Near the end of December, 147, Hasdrubal requested a conference with Scipio's ally and friend, King Gulussa of Numidia. Scipio consented, and Hasdrubal went to the meeting ignorant of the disasters at Nepheris and of Rome's success in stopping an army of Mauretanians coming from Morocco to help Carthage.

The story of the negotiations comes from Polybius, who at that time was with Scipio. Polybius testifies to Hasdrubal's character and personality in describing his behavior and appearance as he met Gulussa.

Hasdrubal had carefully prepared the meeting place. After his brutal treatment of Roman prisoners, he did not know what to expect from the Romans. Hasdrubal's safety was always a primary consideration to Hasdrubal. He arrived wearing a suit of armor, over which he wore a cloak of royal purple. He was guarded by ten swordsmen. Leaving his bodyguard a few paces to the rear, he advanced to a position protected by a trench and palisade almost twenty feet from Gulussa. Then he beckoned to Gulussa to approach. Protocol, of great importance to the Romans, required that Hasdrubal should have gone to Gulussa, but the Numidian king, unpretentious and unsophisticated, advanced without an escort.

In these few sentences Polybius discloses Hasdrubal's vanity, his timidity, and his undiplomatic behavior. The colloquy proceeds:

GULUSSA: Whom are you afraid of that you come here armed from head to foot?

HASDRUBAL: I fear the Romans.

GULUSSA: Then you would not have requested this meeting unless you needed something. What do you want?

HASDRUBAL: I beg you to act as my envoy to the general. I consent on my part to submit to any terms if only the Romans will spare this unhappy city.

GULUSSA: My good friend, you seem to me to make a perfectly childish request. How do you expect, now you are surrounded by land and sea and have almost abandoned all hope of safety, to persuade the Romans to grant you what they refused you, when at the time they were still in Utica, you approached them with your strength yet intact?

HASDRUBAL: You are mistaken, for I still have good hopes of what our foreign allies may do for us. [He did not yet know about Nepheris and the Mauretanians.] We still have resources in the city. We rely on the gods to help us. Surely they will not suffer us to be thus betrayed, but will give us many means of salvation. Beg the general to think of the gods and of Fortune and to spare the city. You may be sure that if we cannot obtain this request, we would all rather be slaughtered than give up the city.

The conference ended. Another meeting was scheduled in three days. When Gulussa reported the conversation and Hasdrubal's request, Scipio laughed sardonically. He spoke scornfully of the Carthaginian and of the atrocities he had committed on Roman prisoners in full view of the Roman army. Then, he said, "after treating our prisoners in such an inhuman manner, now Hasdrubal expects help from the gods after violating even the laws of men."

Gulussa, however, argued for an agreement. War was an uncertain business. Scipio had a chance to end the war with a victory, without further fighting. Then Gulussa used an argument that never failed to convince a Roman commanding general serving the last months of his term of office. The Numidian pointed out that a new consul would arrive before the end of March (146 B.C.) to take over Scipio's command. If the war dragged on, the next commanding general would derive all the glory from Scipio's victory at Nepheris and the Carthaginian surrender which Scipio's siege works were certain to bring about. The new consul, not Scipio, would receive a Roman triumph, the most sought-after honor a Roman citizen could win. Therefore, at a second meeting with Hasdrubal, Gulussa argued, he should return with not only acceptable, but with irresistibly tempting conditions to obtain the surrender of Carthage.

This was sound reasoning. Said Scipio: "Inform Hasdrubal that he [Scipio] answered for the safety of the Carthaginian general, himself, his wife and children, and the families of ten of his friends, and that in addition to this, he might keep ten talents out of his own fortune and take with him any slaves he chose to the number of a hundred."

At the appointed time and place Gulussa arrived with Scipio's offer. Polybius describes the conference and its results:

The Carthaginian again advanced slowly to meet him in great state, wearing his full armour and purple robe, leaving the tyrants of tragedy much to seek. He was by nature corpulent, and he had now become pot-bellied and was unnaturally red in the face, so that it looked as if he were living like a fatted ox in the plenty of a festival, instead of being at the head of a people suffering from such extreme misery that it would be difficult to set it down in words. However, when he met the king and listened to Scipio's offer, slapping his thigh often and calling upon the gods and Fortune, he said that the day would never come on which Hasdrubal would look at the same time on the sun and on his city being consumed by fire; for the most noble funeral for right-minded men was to perish in their native city amid her flames. So that when we look at his utterances we admire the man and his high-souled words, but when we turn to his actual behavior we are amazed by his ignobility and cowardice. For, to begin with, when the rest of the citizens were utterly perishing from famine, he gave drinking parties and offered his guests sumptuous second courses and by his own good cheer exposed the general distress. For the number of deaths was incredibly large and so was the number of daily desertions due to famine. And next by making mock of some and inflicting outrage and death on others he terrorized the populace and maintained his authority in his sorely stricken country by means to which a tyrant in a prosperous city would scarcely resort.

That day Hasdrubal spoke like a man. He knew what the offer meant. He could escape with his family and friends. But the rest of the Carthaginians would be put to the sword or sold into slavery, and the city would be wiped out. With theatrical gestures he spurned the offer.

Scipio now decided that armed force must end Carthaginian resistance. He opened the attack in early March from his bridgehead on the Choma. The commercial and naval harbors called the Cothon must be captured first. Next would come an assault on the wall between the harbors and the city and finally on the strongest ramparts of all—those surrounding the Byrsa. Hasdrubal, hopeless of preventing a breakthrough into the fortified rectangular inner commercial harbor, fired the ship stores, the ships, and the buildings in the area.

Scipio in person commanded the assault on the offensive's left flank. The flames of the Cothon blocked his men; but Laelius, on the right, found that the Carthaginians were not keeping close watch on his front. His men scaled the walls around the circular naval base. The Carthaginians, weak with hunger and greatly outnumbered, resisted only feebly. The wall between the two harbors and the city was quickly taken. By nightfall the Romans had penetrated into the city of Carthage as far as the Forum lying north of the inner harbor. There Scipio and his army passed the night.

At dawn, four thousand fresh troops reinforced the tired fighters of the previous day. Appian reports concerning these new arrivals:

They entered the temple of Apollo [near or on the Forum], whose statue was there, covered with gold, in a shrine of beaten gold, weighing 1000 talents, which they plundered, chopping it with their swords and disregarding the commands of their officers until they had divided it among themselves, after which they returned to their duty.

When booty was to be had, even Scipio could not always control his troops.

Scipio's last military objective was the summit of the Byrsa, where Dido's men had stretched the oxhide ribbon not quite 668 years before. The anniversary was almost at hand. The morning after the destruction of the statue of Apollo, Scipio stood in the Forum, at the foot of the hill, with thousands of Roman legionaries thirsting for revenge and plunder.

Scipio looked up at the awe-inspiring walls and towers on the Byrsa. Above the ramparts rose the Temple of Eshmoun, which, we may conjecture, resembled the Temple of Solomon that Tyrian architects designed for Jerusalem at the Hebrew king's behest.

Scipio could have had no illusions about the terrifying difficulties of his last assault. Only three streets, winding steeply around the hill, led to its summit. Scipio knew these three streets and their tall structures would canalize his attacks, facilitating defense. He knew he would have to pay an exorbitant price for this hilltop. His will was indomitable, but he knew the Carthaginian soldiers also had indomitable wills, and the nine hundred Roman deserters serving with them knew that capture meant crucifixion. They would not sell a square inch of the approaches to the sacred enclosures for less than their lives.

Appian describes the position on the Byrsa as "the strongest part of the city." It had become the refuge for as many inhabitants as could crowd into it. On both sides of the three streets the tall buildings stood wall to wall, except where alleys separated one block of buildings from another. Many residents—old people, women, and children—still lived there. But Carthaginian soldiers turned each building into a fort. They fought from each floor; they hurled missiles from the roofs into the Roman cohorts on the streets.

The Romans first broke into the buildings closest to the Forum, eventually killing all their occupants—civilians and soldiers alike. Then with picks and shovels and crowbars they cut a passage into the next house. When they had reached a roof, they moved on to the next one, fighting every inch of the way. When they came to the alleys, they bridged the gap with planks.

The advance, day by day, was measured in feet and yards. Behind the Roman advance lay shattered buildings and piles of rubble so high that Scipio had to organize detachments to clear a path for food, weapons, and reinforcements bound for the front line.

The horrors exceeded those of the usual battlefield. Civilians, young and old, suffered unpremeditated atrocities when they got in the path of the troops fighting in their homes, on the roofs, and in the streets. Groans and shrieks from the wounded and dying mingled with the cries of attackers and defenders as they came face to face.

For six days and six nights the struggle raged. When finally Scipio reached the walls of the Byrsa, he ordered the torch put to the buildings which had impeded him.

Appian, in a paragraph definitely not for the squeamish, writes:

Then came new scenes of horror. The fire spread and carried everything down, and the soldiers did not wait to destroy the buildings little by little, but pulled them all down together. So the crashing grew louder, and many fell with the stones into the midst of the dead. Others were seen still living, especially old men, women, and young children who had hidden in the in-

most nooks of the houses, some of them wounded, some more or less burned, and uttering horrible cries. Still others, thrust out and falling from such a height with the stones, timbers, and fire, were torn asunder into all kinds of horrible shapes, crushed and mangled. Nor was this the end of their miseries, for the street cleaners, who were removing the rubbish with axes, mattocks, and boat-hooks, and making the roads passable, tossed with these instruments the dead and the living together into holes in the ground, sweeping them along like sticks and stones or turning them over with their iron tools, and man was used for filling up a ditch. Some were thrown in head foremost, while their legs, sticking out of the ground, writhed a long time. Others fell with their feet downward and their heads above ground. Horses ran over them, crushing their faces and skulls, not purposely on the part of the riders, but in their headlong haste. Nor did the street cleaners either do these things on purpose; but the press of war, the glory of approaching victory, the rush of the soldiery, the confused noise of heralds and trumpeters all around, the tribunes and centurions changing guard and marching the cohorts hither and thither—all together made everybody frantic and heedless of the spectacle before their eyes.

Scipio faced more such days; he had to set fire to the remainder of the city which the Senate had ordered him to destroy. He had slept little for six days and six nights. He sat down on a high place to supervise the clearing of the streets to the Byrsa and to direct preparations for the attack on the citadel. Suddenly one of the Byrsa's gates opened. A delegation, bearing olive branches, moved slowly to Scipio's feet. Kneeling, they prayed that Scipio would spare the lives of all who were willing to depart as prisoners of war from the Byrsa. This he granted to all except the Roman deserters. A pathetic crowd of thirty-six thousand men and women came out of a narrow gate in the wall. Scipio furnished them with a guard to protect them.

The Roman deserters, despairing of their lives, had sought safety in the walled enclosure of the temple of Eshmoun (Aesculapius) with Hasdrubal and his wife and his sons. They defended themselves for hours. Finally, overcome by hunger, sleeplessness, fear, and weariness, they abandoned the enclosure and fled to the temple roof.

Hasdrubal and his men had resisted desperately. Hasdrubal with his wife and children thus far had kept his promise not to surrender. From the roof of the temple, he looked down on the flaming city. His courage failed. He deserted his wife and children. He deserted his men. He

secretly fled to Scipio, bearing an olive branch. Scipio commanded him to sit at his feet and there showed him to the deserters. When they saw him, they asked silence, and when it was granted, they heaped all manner of reproaches upon Hasdrubal, then set fire to the temple and were consumed in it. It is said that as the fire was lighted the wife of Hasdrubal, in full view of Scipio, arraying herself as best she could amid such disaster, and setting her children by her side, said, so as to be heard by Scipio: "For you, Romans, the gods have no cause of indignation, since you exercise the right of war. But upon this Hasdrubal, betrayer of his country and her temples, of me and his children, may the gods of Carthage take vengeance, and you be their instrument." Then, turning to Hasdrubal, "Wretch," she exclaimed, "traitor, most cowardly of men, the fire will entomb me and my children. But as for you, what Roman triumph will you, the leader of great Carthage, decorate? Ah, what punishment will you not receive from him at whose feet you are now sitting." Having reproached him thus, she slew her children, flung them into the fire, and plunged in after them. With these words, it is said, did the wife of Hasdrubal die, as Hasdrubal should have died himself.

So died Carthage, the city that had tempted Alcibiades, Agathocles, Alexander the Great, Pyrrhus, and Regulus.

172

How mighty was the city which was destroyed is shown, to mention only a single fact, by the long duration of the fire; for it was only after seventeen days of continual effort that the flames were with difficulty put out which the enemy had themselves kindled in their houses and temples, in order that, since the city could not be saved from the Romans, the material for a triumph might be burnt.

Scipio was moved as he gazed upon what he had wrought. In one of his most eloquent paragraphs, Appian writes:

Scipio, beholding this city which had flourished 700 years from its foundation, and had ruled over so many lands, islands, and seas, as rich in arms and fleets, elephants and money as the mightiest empires, but far surpassing them in reckless courage and in readiness to act [when aroused]—since, when stripped of all its ships and arms, it had sustained famine and a mighty war for three years—now come to its end in total destruction; Scipio, beholding this spectacle, is said to have shed tears and publicly lamented the fortune of the enemy. After meditating by himself a long time and reflecting on the inevitable fall of cities, nations, and empires as well as of individuals; upon the fate of Troy, that once proud city; upon the fate of the Assyrian, the Median, and afterwards of the great Persian empire, and most recently of all, of the splendid Macedonian empire; either voluntarily or otherwise the words of the poet escaped his lips:

> "The day shall come in which our sacred Troy
> And Priam, and the people over whom
> Spear-bearing Priam rules, shall perish all."

Being asked by Polybius in familiar conversation (for Polybius had been his tutor) what he meant by using these words, Polybius says that he did not hesitate frankly to name his own country, for whose fate he feared when he considered the mutability of human affairs. And Polybius wrote this down just as he heard it.

173

XIX

ROME VICTORIOUS

Scipio's first thought—after he had ceased to weep for Carthage —was to cheer war-weary Rome with the tidings of victory. He knew how much Rome needed the good news after three years of frustration and humiliation by an enemy that had begun fighting without a weapon. He loaded a swift warship with spoils to bear witness to Carthage's fall and ordered the captain to make all speed to the Tiber. Then he turned to some other pressing business. He gave his soldiers permission to pillage—the prize they had so long awaited. He paraded his legions to decorate and reward the centurions and legionaries who had distinguished themselves in combat, but, in the interest of discipline, pointedly withheld medals and cash bonuses from those who had violated the shrine of Apollo.

In authorizing plunder, Scipio made some exceptions. He reserved to the state all gold and silver and all the lavish votive offerings in the temples. In a gesture to the erstwhile Greek cities in Sicily, long since a Roman province, he permitted them to claim any statues or other temple ornaments they could identify as booty taken by the Carthaginians in their wars with those cities. Finally, the time had come to give thanks to the gods for victory:

He conducted a ceremony in honor of Mars and Minerva. His homage to them was a holocaust of captured weapons and Carthaginian ships.

When the ship bearing the news from Scipio tied up on the

riverbank below Rome's Capitol, the quiet April evening took on the appearance of the December carnival of the Saturnalia. Appian describes the occasion:

> When the people of Rome saw the ship and heard of the victory early in the evening, they poured into the streets and spent the whole night congratulating and embracing each other like people just now delivered from some great fear, just now confirmed in their supremacy, just now assured of the permanence of their own city, and winners of such a victory as they had never won before.... They knew of no other war which had so terrified them at their own gates as the Punic Wars. . . . Remembering these things, they were so excited over this victory that they could hardly believe it, and they asked each other if it was really true that Carthage was destroyed. And so they conversed the whole night, telling how the arms of the Carthaginians had been taken away from them, and how at once, contrary to expectations, they supplied themselves with others; how they lost their ships and built a great fleet out of old material; how the mouth of their harbor was closed, yet they managed to open another in a few days. . . . Thus did the Romans pass the night.

The next day they gave thanks to their gods, with sacrifices and ceremonial pomp, and with games and spectacles.

No peace treaty followed the Third Punic War. None was needed, for there was no one with whom to conclude it.

Rome sent ten of the noblest members of the Senate "to arrange the affairs of Africa in conjunction with Scipio, to the advantage of Rome." Utica was rewarded with additional territory, but what power did she enjoy and for how long? Not a word was said about the Numidians whose forty years of proxy warfare had done so much to make Roman victory possible. Masinissa's dream of a Numidian empire stretching from Mauretania to Egypt was dead. Carthage as a Roman province blocked Numidian expansion eastward. (But, a little over thirty years later,

Jugurtha, a grandnephew of Masinissa, led Numidia in a long, hard war against Rome. In those years, it took longer for allies to become enemies.)

Rome had fought the Second and the Third Punic Wars for world dominion. She had won, she had eliminated Carthage as a threat, and had put her foot in the door of Africa. And just to make sure, the senatorial delegation ordered that "if anything was still left of Carthage, Scipio should raze it to the ground, and that nobody should be allowed to live there." Scipio obeyed orders. He buried Carthage. No one would ever resuscitate it. The site of Carthage was declared accursed and, until Julius Caesar authorized it a century later, nobody dared violate the curse. Towns that had supported Carthage suffered the same fate as the capital city. Frightfulness was Rome's chief weapon in 146.

To give her strategy of terror added emphasis in the minds of her future victims, Rome also destroyed Corinth in Greece. Is it a mere coincidence that Carthage and Corinth, two of the world's wealthiest and most famous commercial cities of antiquity, two cities occupying geographical positions of the utmost importance in Mediterranean trade, were destroyed in 146 B.C.? If Rome did not fight these wars for economic reasons, as most modern historians believe, she could not have failed to profit from eliminating their commercial rivalry on the sea. In any event, taxation of the Roman people would be decreased: The final act of the senatorial delegation was to impose an annual real estate and personal property tax on both men and women living within the former Carthaginian boundaries which henceforth was to be governed by a Roman praetor. For Rome, war certainly paid its way.

And Scipio? What of his future? Rome gave him the "most glorious triumph that had ever been known, splendid with gold and crowned with all the statues and votive offerings that the Carthaginians had gathered from all parts of the world during their long period of continuous victories."

There can be little doubt that Hasdrubal walked at the head of the band of prisoners who in a triumph were always exhibited to the Roman populace lining the Via Sacra. But when the procession was about to climb the Capitoline Hill, Scipio did not carry out the usual ceremony at that point. He did not halt the procession and have Hasdrubal led into the adjoining prison to be put to death. According to Zonaras, Hasdrubal spent the rest of his life in Italy "in honorable confinement," i.e., unfettered and on parole. He had to live with his conscience—and his memories.

The thirty-six thousand Carthaginians who surrendered were sold into slavery. At least one hundred thousand others must have died of disease or starvation during the siege. The comparatively few survivors who escaped slavery lived henceforth in a Roman province and nobody was concerned over them. And although "the ruin of Carthage is indeed considered to have been the greatest of calamities," a non-Carthaginian could take a philosophical view of it. Polybius writes with the imperturbability of the onlooker that "the Carthaginians, having been utterly exterminated by the calamity which overtook them, were for the future insensible of their sufferings." The dead feel no pain.

But no Roman writer offers more than the feeblest defense of his country in this crime of the ages. Polybius, however, assures us that in Greece there was no unanimity of opinion.

He begins with the opinion of

some Greeks who approved the action of the Romans, saying that they had taken wise and statesmanlike measures in defense of their empire. For to destroy this source of perpetual menace, this city which had constantly disputed the supremacy with them and was still able to dispute it if it had the opportunity and thus to secure the dominion of their own country, was the act of intelligent and far-seeing men.

The fallacy of course is that Rome, during the 120 years of conflict, was invariably the aggressor.

Another Greek view cited by Polybius places the responsibility for the Third Punic War squarely on Rome's "lust of domination like that of Athens and Sparta." And a third shows that the ancients recognized the chicanery of a cold war as well as we do today. Greeks who advanced this view began by admitting

that the Romans were, generally speaking, a civilized people. . . .
BUT IN THE PRESENT CASE, THROUGHOUT THE WHOLE OF THEIR PRO-
CEEDINGS IN REGARD TO CARTHAGE, THEY HAD USED DECEIT AND FRAUD,
OFFERING CERTAIN THINGS ONE AT A TIME AND KEEPING OTHERS SE-
CRET, UNTIL THEY CUT OFF EVERY HOPE THE CITY HAD OF HELP FROM
HER ALLIES. THIS, THEY SAID, WAS MORE THE INTRIGUE OF A DICTATOR
THAN THE DELIBERATE PLAN OF A CIVILIZED STATE SUCH AS ROME. IT
COULD ONLY BE JUSTLY DESCRIBED AS SOMETHING VERY LIKE IMPIETY
AND TREACHERY. [Emphasis mine. D.A.]

Finally Polybius reports the view of still other Greeks that, after Carthage surrendered unconditionally, Rome had the right to do what she wanted with Carthage. This view, of course, forgets Rome's promise to preserve the freedom and autonomy of Carthage. We can only regret that Polybius did not give his own view of the situation as he stated it concerning Rome's declaration of war in 238. That time he did not hesitate to call it a war without "any reasonable pretext or cause" and "contrary to all justice."

The visitor to Carthage today finds hardly a trace of the Phoenician city amid the modern villas in that suburb of Tunis. Side by side with the remains of the Roman theater and odeon, the amphitheater and the public baths—built after Julius Caesar lifted the curse on the site—are the remains of the churches of early Christian Carthage. The American ambassador lives just below the Byrsa. From the Byrsa's summit, the visitor sees the United States flag flying beside the ambassador's villa under the hill where the Carthaginians made their last stand in defense of their homes and their freedom. A few miles away, in the Megara, where once lived the wealthy families of Carthage in their villas and palaces behind the city's ramparts, lies a cemetery for American dead of World War II who gave their lives for their country throughout North Africa, once part of the Carthaginian empire, fitting comrades in death of the scores of thousands who died nearby to keep Carthage free.

On the Byrsa, we may do homage, not to a single unknown soldier, but to the unknown and nameless people of the city and empire of Carthage who deserve this epitaph:

Nothing in their life became them like the leaving it.

XX

THE ANATOMY OF CONQUEST

The destruction of Carthage has lessons for the Free World today. Communist Russia and China, like republican Rome, are spurred by visions of grandeur, the urge to win dominion of the world. Can we profit from the disaster which befell Carthage? Fortunately we do not suffer in the United States from most of the maladies that so weakened Carthage. But as a warning of dangers, the fall of Carthage is salutary history indeed, and those who forget history are doomed to relive it.

Carthage fell after a prolonged conflict between a would-be world conqueror and the chief obstacle in its path. Carthage was that obstacle to Rome. The United States is that obstacle to the Soviet Union and Communist China. The word in Rome was "wipe out" the enemy; in Moscow the word is "bury"; in Peking the United States "can never avert its doom."

Carthage was no isolated case. Creeping aggression backed by militaristic ruthlessness has succeeded many times in the past. Appeasement does not prevent war, it assures conflict.

The chief difference between a hot war and a cold war is that a cold war, like a chess game, is a long-drawn-out struggle in which luck plays little or no part. The relative skill—and equally important, the will to win—of the players determines whose king is checkmated.

In a cold war, one of the two opponents, the aggressor, is determined to win by careful planning, wise moves, and ruthless deception. Victory is to be his by fair means or foul. If the victim does not understand the game, the loss of a pawn here or a knight there does not worry him. If his thoughts are elsewhere, he does not see the traps set for him by his opponent. If his will to win is insufficient, his strength is gradually eroded until, when the tide of combat goes clearly against him, he discovers too late that the price of defeat is intolerably high.

Rome did not invent the cold war. More than a century and a half before Rome began applying this subtle form of aggression, Philip of Macedon used subversion, psychological warfare, deception, and salami tactics to reduce to impotence Athens and other Greek city-states. Nor did all of Rome's actions follow a careful blueprint of conquest. Some moves were merely logical responses to immediate circumstances. Rome may not have known the scientific basis of psychological warfare, but this did not lessen for Carthage the destructive consequences of Roman terror, cat-and-mouse tactics, and shifting from a hard to a soft line.

Throughout history, the anatomy of the cold war varies little.

First there is the basic cause: the lust for power and glory and domination by a man or an oligarchy.

Second there is the character of the man or oligarchy. He or it must have indomitable will to reach the goal, caution and rashness, frightfulness, and pretended gentleness in turn to deceive and baffle the victim.

Third is the *strategy of the indirect* approach which avoids decisive war until the victim has been weakened sufficiently by deception, psychological war, subversion, and, when possible, by proxy powers such as Numidia to ensure the conqueror's physical and moral superiority. The conqueror seizes and keeps the initiative. Like the Roman consuls in camp near Utica, who "did not unmask all their demands at once, fearing that if the Carthaginians learned them in season, they would enter upon war with their resources undiminished," a conqueror proceeds slowly, backs out of a tight situation, and by a gradual approach, lulls the victim into attrition by appeasement and acceptance.

Fourth is the *character of the victim*, usually wealthy, materialistic, peace-loving, disposed toward appeasement and irresolute in outlook. The primary goal of the victim is maintenance of the *status quo* and "business-as-usual." The victim is usually weak-willed, beset by internal dissension, and undermined by a strong peace-at-any-price faction.

If history teaches one lesson which is unchallengeable, this is the truth of Vegetius's exhortation: *"Qui desiderat pacem, praeparat bellum."*

APPENDIXES

1

THE SOURCES

Sources for Carthaginian history after Hannibal's defeat at the battle of Zama are extremely limited. The only contemporary historian who observed the last stage of the Third Punic War was Polybius (203–120 B.C.).

Polybius, a native of a Greek city-state in the Peloponnese, was one of a thousand Greek hostages who reached Rome after the Roman defeat of the Greek army in 167 B.C. (Battle of Pydna). He was a well-educated, highly cultured man with much military and political experience. He became an honored member of an aristocratic Roman intellectual group who loved and admired Greek civilization. In time he was made the tutor of the young Roman who would destroy Carthage in 146 and who is known as Scipio Africanus the Younger. His history of Rome sought to explain how Rome conquered and dominated the world in the years from 264 to the destruction of Carthage in 146.

Polybius did not let his admiration of Rome's constitution and her rise to empire prevent him from writing impartial history. Describing the beginning of the battle of Zama in 202 B.C. he said, "the Carthaginians [were] fighting for their own safety and the dominion of Africa, and the Romans for the empire of the world." He did not hesitate to state that the war declared by Rome against Carthage in 238—which I call the unnumbered, unfought Punic War—was without "any reasonable pretext or cause" and that Carthage's loss of Sardinia was "contrary to all justice." Other evidence of his objectivity can be cited, and is observed also in the accounts of later historians who depended on him for events of the Punic Wars.

185

Polybius wrote a history of forty books of which only the first five are intact. Fragments and excerpts of other books have reached us, but for the period of the last half century of Carthage very little has been salvaged. This is unfortunate because Polybius accompanied Scipio in 146 during the agony and fall of Carthage.

Certainly later historians followed Polybius's account of the Third Punic War. Internal evidence supports the view that Appian, a Greek historian and a Roman official, who lived about A.D. 150, adheres closely to Polybius. Appian's description of the Third Punic War is the only fairly complete account of that war and fortunately it is the best book of his Roman history. Appian is neither a distinguished nor always a reliable historian, but there is less reason to question the accuracy of his *Punic Wars* than other portions of his work.

Despite his Roman point of view, Appian does not fail to record Roman deception in Masinissa's seizure of Carthaginian territory. More noteworthy, however, is his admission when writing about Rome's anxiety after two years of frustration in the last Punic War (149–148 B.C.) that "there could be no expectation of peace since they [i.e., the Romans] had been the first to break faith."

Other sources of value are Livy (59 B.C.–A.D. 17), whose voluminous history of Rome was written to glorify his native land and is frequently prejudiced and sometimes even false. His books on the Third Punic War are also lost, and only summaries of them survive. In one summary, Livy does go so far as to admit, when discussing Rome's order in 149 B.C. to Carthage to build a new city ten miles from the sea, that "By their unworthy treatment they drove the Carthaginians to war."

The works of Plutarch (born A.D. 50), Diodorus Siculus (about 40 B.C.), and Strabo (64 B.C.–A.D. 19) provide additional information about the final fifty years of Carthaginian history. The authors cited are all available in the Loeb Classical Library which publishes the Greek or Latin text facing the English translation.

2

CARTHAGINIAN NAMES

An explanation of the word Punic may be desirable since I have
been asked more than once, "Who were the Punes?" The word
goes back to the Greeks, who called the people living in the
city-states of Tyre, Sidon, and kindred cities in the area of
modern Lebanon, "Phoinikoi." The Greek word for a deep red
color is "phoinix," the color of the famous dye discovered in
Tyre and exploited in Phoenician commerce. The Romans later
turned the Greek word into Latin, calling the Phoenicians the
"Poeni." The Latin adjective *punicus* gives us the English word.

But if "Punic" puzzles some people, the Carthaginian system
of naming individuals confuses everybody. Take, for example, the
name "Hasdrubal," which in Phoenician means "My help is
Baal," Baal (Lord in English) being the Phoenician sun-god of
fertility. Carthaginian history records eight generals named Hasdrubal, of whom five served in the Second and Third Punic
War period as follows:

SECOND PUNIC WAR

Hasdrubal, son-in-law of Hamilcar, date of birth unknown.
Commanded in Spain for eight years until his assassination in
220 B.C.

Hasdrubal, son of Hamilcar, killed in the battle of the Metaurus while leading reinforcements to his brother, Hannibal, in Italy, 207 B.C.

Hasdrubal, son of Gisgo, defeated with his ally Syphax in 204. Father of Sophonisba.

Hasdrubal, leader of Carthaginian army in the disastrous campaign of 150 B.C. against Masinissa. Commanded force near Nepheris in first year of last Punic War, and commander of defenses of Carthage from 148 to 146.

Hasdrubal (Numidianus), the surname added by author to distinguish him from the other Hasdrubal. A grandson of Masinissa through a daughter married to a Carthaginian. Murdered at instigation of the other Hasdrubal in 148.

Hannibals are numerous, but not so confusing. In this book Hannibal always designates the eldest son of Hamilcar, the great leader of the Second Punic War. The meaning of his name is "the favor of Baal." Another Hannibal of the last decade of Carthage has a distinguishing surname, "the Starling."

Sophonisba is the Latin way of writing the Phoenician name Sophanbaal, which apparently means "my guardian is Baal." Actually Livy calls her Sophoniba. She was the daughter of Hasdrubal, son of Gisgo.

The three foregoing names with the last syllable being Baal or the Lord show the deeply religious spirit of the Carthaginians. Another god, Melkart, appears in the following names:

Hamilcar, too, occurs more than once in Carthaginian history. In this book we are concerned almost exclusively with the Hamilcar Barca, who is one of the few Carthaginians who had a surname. Hamilcar means "servant of Melkart," the tutelary divinity of Tyre. Barca means "lightning." One other Hamilcar appears in this book but he also has a surname, "the Samnite."

Phameas, the cavalry commander of the last Punic War, whom the younger Scipio persuaded to desert Carthage, has a name that sounds as if it were of Greek origin. We know nothing of him except his bold and skillful tactics and his surrender to Scipio. Perhaps, like Xanthippus of the First Punic War, he was a Spartan soldier of fortune, or a descendant of such a *condottiere*. In Livy's *Summaries* (Vol. XIV, Loeb Library, p. 33), he is called "Phameas Himilco," "a brave man who was of extraordinary service to the Carthaginians." Himilco means "favor of Melkart," so it is tempting to guess that he might have been the off-spring of a marriage of a Carthaginian and a Greek. Appian never gives him the surname Himilco, which was a well-known Carthaginian name, and I have followed Appian's usage.

Mago, the youngest son of Hamilcar, who fought with his brother Hannibal at the Trebia and carried the news of Cannae to Carthage, has a name seemingly derived from the famous Magonid family, the most powerful politically throughout Carthaginian history.

3

CHRONOLOGY

(All dates B.C.)

1100   Phoenicians found Utica in North Africa and Cadiz in Spain. (Traditional dates.)

814   Tyrians found Carthage (traditional date). (See Carpenter, Rhys, in bibliography concerning first two dates.)

800–700   Greeks colonize South Italy and Sicily.

753   Rome founded (traditional date).

600–268   Intermittent war between Carthage and Greek city-states in Sicily.

508   First Rome–Carthage commercial treaty.

480   Greeks defeat Carthaginians at Himera in northern Sicily.

332   Alexander the Great besieges Tyre.

310–307   Agathocles of Syracuse invades Carthage.

279   Alliance of Carthage and Rome against King Pyrrhus of Epirus.

278   Pyrrhus invades Sicily.

THE PUNIC WARS

264   First Punic War begins.

256–255   Regulus invades Carthage and suffers defeat.

241   Carthaginian fleet destroyed off western Sicily. Carthage surrenders and loses possessions in Sicily.

241–238	Revolt of Carthaginian mercenaries aided by Libyans and Numidians.
238	Rome declares war on helpless Carthage which immediately surrenders with loss of Sardinia, etc.
237	Hamilcar Barca, with his son Hannibal, goes to Spain.
221	Hannibal in his twenty-sixth year made commander in Spain.
218	Rome declares war on Carthage, beginning the Second Punic War. Hannibal from his Spanish base invades Italy via the Alps. Battle of the Trebia. Rome invades Spain.
217	Battle of Lake Trasimene.
216	Battle of Cannae. Revolt of Capua from Rome.
215	Philip V of Macedon forms alliance with Hannibal.
214	Revolt of Syracuse from Rome.
212	Rome recovers Syracuse.
211	Rome recovers Capua. Roman defeats in Spain.
210	P. Cornelius Scipio commander in Spain.
204	Scipio invades Carthaginian territory.
202	Hannibal recalled, defeated at battle of Zama.
201	Peace treaty ends Second Punic War. Carthage reduced to its territory in Africa and forced to pay huge indemnity.
195	Hannibal flees Carthage to avoid Roman imprisonment.
193	Masinissa, king of Numidia, commences progressive seizure of Carthaginian territory with Roman connivance.
191	Carthage offers to pay entire balance of war indemnity.
191–151	Numidia, a buffer state, becomes a proxy power.
154	Tribes in area of modern Portugal and Spain begin prolonged rebellion against Roman rule. Carthalo with Carthaginian mercenaries raids territory seized and occupied by Masinissa.
153	Cato comes to Carthage. Urges Roman Senate to destroy Carthage. Despite Nasica's appeal against Cato, Senate

decides on ultimate war. (Note: This date is uncertain and varies in our sources from 157 to 150. The logic of events suggests that Cato's visit occurred in 153.)

152   Nasica heads another Roman commission to Carthage which for the first time settles dispute in favor of Carthage.

151–150   Masinissa besieges Carthaginian town of Oroscopa. In winter Carthage declares war on Masinissa in violation of treaty of 201.

150   Carthage mobilizes army under Hasdrubal to relieve Oroscopa.

Pitched battle with Masinissa, victory to neither side. After long siege of his camp Hasdrubal surrenders army, which is annihilated.

Rome starts mobilization.

Carthaginian embassy to Rome denies government's responsibility for war on Masinissa.

Rome refuses to accept explanation.

4

SUGGESTED CHRONOLOGY

OF FINAL PUNIC WAR

149
March   Second Carthaginian embassy rebuffed in Rome.

Utica defects and offers Rome city and its ports for base in war against Carthage.

Rome declares war on Carthage.

Roman expeditionary force sails for Utica via Lily-baeum in Sicily with secret orders to raze city of Carthage.

April 1   Third Carthaginian peace delegation to Rome agrees to unconditional surrender.

12   Three hundred hostages delivered to Roman army in Sicily.

16   Roman army lands in Utica.

20   Roman consuls in Utica demand unilateral disarmament.

28   Carthage delivers all armament to consul at Utica.

30   Roman consuls divulge their secret orders to destroy Carthage.

Carthage declares war on Rome, secures loyal support of Hasdrubal and his army outside the walls, and appoints a grandson of Masinissa, also named Hasdrubal, to command city's defenses.

May 15   First Roman assault on Carthage's walls repulsed.

18   Second Roman assault fails.

19	Consuls strengthen fortifications of their camp.
23–28	Censorinus seeks timber for battering rams and siege equipment.
	Phameas raids Roman working parties.
31	Third Roman assault on walls fails.
June 1–30	Battering rams, etc., completed, and area on Taenia prepared and road built.
July 1–5	Battering rams emplaced.
6–10	Battering rams demolish section of wall.
	Assault force fails to enter city.
	Carthaginians counterattack battering rams which are damaged beyond repair.
11	Romans make violent assault through breach which is repulsed.
26	Dog Star rises.
Aug. 1	Censorinus moves camp to the Taenia.
10	Fire ships attack Roman fleet.
20	Censorinus returns to Rome.
25	Carthaginian night attack on Manilius fails.
25–31	Manilius strengthens his camp defenses.
Sept. 1–20	Phameas's raids continue against Roman foragers.
25	Carthaginian night attack from the city on naval defense camp. Scipio's stratagem forces Carthaginian withdrawal.
Oct. 10	Hasdrubal defeats Manilius in battle of Nepheris.
11	Scipio rescues the lost cohorts.
Nov. 15–16	Manilius marches up the hill and down again on the field of Nepheris without engaging Hasdrubal.

148	
Jan. 30	Phameas surrenders to Scipio who some weeks later accompanies the Carthaginian traitor to Rome.
Mar. 30	Calpurnius Piso and L. Mancinus, the new consuls, relieve Manilius.

Begins year of successful Carthaginian defensive resistance.

Rome fights wars on two fronts: i.e., Carthage and Macedonia which she defeats later this year. Rebellion also in Spain.

Apr.–May Roman siege of Clupea on Cape Bon fails.

June Carthage offers to aid Macedonia.

June–Sept. Siege of Bizerte also fails.

July Hasdrubal Numidianus, commanding in the city, murdered following charges of treason by Hasdrubal, commander at Nepheris.

Winter P. Cornelius Scipio Aemilianus elected consul in Rome.

147

Mar. 23 Scipio sails with reinforcements for Carthage.

Apr. 2 Mancinus assaults Carthage's northern wall.

3 Scipio arrives in Utica and rescues Mancinus.

5–30 Scipio restores order and discipline in demoralized Roman army.

May 1–2 Scipio withdraws from Megara after penetrating Carthage's defenses.

3–30 Scipio constructs fortified camp across isthmus, completely blocking land approach to Carthage.

June 1–Sept. 15 Mole blocking entrance to Carthage's ports completed; all land and sea communication with besieged city finally shut off.

June 15–Sept. 10 Carthage secretly builds fleet.

Sept. 11 Carthaginian fleet surprises Romans through channel, cut through sea-front of fortifications.

14 Carthaginian–Roman fleets fight their last battle.

18 Scipio attacks Choma with battering rams from mole.

19 Carthaginian night attack destroys Roman equipment.

Oct. 10   Romans capture Choma.

20–30   Roman siege and capture of fortified Carthaginian camp near Nepheris.

Nov. 25   Nepheris surrenders.

Dec.   Meetings of Hasdrubal and King Gulussa of Numidia.

146

Mar.   Final Roman attacks seize the two ports and the Byrsa.

Hasdrubal surrenders and Carthage is razed to the ground.

RECOMMENDED READING

CARPENTER, RHYS. "Phoenicians in the West." *American Journal of Archaeology*, Vol. 62, No. 1, Jan. 1958. This distinguished scholar argues on archaeological evidence that Greeks preceded Phoenicians in the western Mediterranean, suggesting later dates than the traditional for the founding of Carthage, Utica, and Cadiz.

CHARLES-PICARD, GILBERT AND COLETTE. *Daily Life in Carthage.* New York, The Macmillan Company, 1961. An authoritative and readable study of Carthaginian history, society, and archaeology translated from the French.

DODGE, LIEUT. COL. THEODORE A. *Hannibal.* Boston, Houghton Mifflin & Co., 1893. The most valuable military study of the Second Punic War.

HARDEN, DONALD. *The Phoenicians.* New York, Frederick A. Praeger, 1962. A distinguished social, political, and cultural history of the Phoenicians with special consideration of the Carthaginians.

LAMB, HAROLD. *Hannibal: One Man Against Rome.* New York, Doubleday. 1958. A very well-written and accurate story of the Second Punic War.

WARMINGTON, B. H. *Carthage.* New York, Frederick A. Praeger, 1960. An excellent comprehensive history of Carthage by a well-known British authority on the early history of North Africa.

RECOMMENDED READING

The following are available only in French:

DUVAL, GENERAL R. *L'enceinte de Carthage*. Comptes Rendus de l'Academie des Inscriptions et Belles Lettres. 1950. A brief but important article describing General Duval's discovery of the Carthaginian main defense line on the isthmus.

GSELL, STEPHANE. *Histoire Ancienne de l'Afrique du Nord*. Paris, Hachette, 1928. Volumes I–IV. The basic and most authoritative study of Carthage and its empire. Required reading for the specialist in this area.

WALTER, GERARD. *La Destruction de Carthage*. Paris, Editions Albin Michel. A full-length history of Carthage which in the author's words is a "very characteristic example of the destruction by force of a state incapable of resisting an adversary superior in vital energy."

INDEX